"J. A. Baker's *The Peregrine* is fift written yesterday. In the half cen little book has only tightened its uncannily prophetic: of the Anth which human activity is now the dominant influence on the environment), of extinction events, of dark ecology—even of virtual reality."
—Robert Macfarlane, *The Guardian*, revisiting *The Peregrine* in 2017

"A most incredible book. It has prose of the caliber that we have not seen since Joseph Conrad.... Whoever really loves literature, whoever really loves movies, should read that book.... [Baker's writing is] almost like a transubstantiation, like in religion, where the observer becomes almost the object—in this case the falcon—he observes.... It's a wonderful, wonderful book." —Werner Herzog

"Darkly poetic.... This is a book about the poetry of death and loss as much as it is about hawks." —Helen Macdonald, author of *H Is for Hawk*

"The book is fervently, strangely alive.... The poet Gerard Manley Hopkins comes to mind ... so does Emily Dickinson, and Virginia Woolf's later novels, especially *The Waves*.... His visual descriptions are mimetic—as if the reader's eye on the page followed a painter's brush, the falcon reeling and refracted in sunlight painted by Tintoretto, in falling darkness by Rouault." —Cynthia Zarin, *The New Yorker*'s Page-Turner blog

"[*The Peregrine*] is the best nature book I've ever read. And you'll want to read it, too, if you have any interest in nature, or birds, or simply in beautiful prose.... I know of no naturalist or scientist who writes better." —Jerry Coyne, author of *Why Evolution Is True*

"Few books have struck me as profoundly as this one. Baker's prose and talent for observation are so penetrating that I deliberately left off reading *The Peregrine* with one page left. This way I can always say I'm reading it rather than have read it." —Stephen Sparks, owner, Point Reyes Books, Point Reyes Station, California

JOHN ALEC BAKER (1926–1987) was born and lived in Essex, England. He left school at the age of sixteen and worked at the Automobile Association and later for the soft drink company Britvic. He was forty-one when he published his first book, *The Peregrine*, the culmination of what he described as a ten-year fascination with hawks. *The Peregrine* won the prestigious Duff Cooper Prize for nonfiction writing in 1968 and was followed in 1969 by *The Hill of Summer*, an exploration of the natural history of Baker's native region. Baker's worsening rheumatoid arthritis curtailed his explorations into the wilderness, and his second book was his last.

ROBERT MACFARLANE's *Mountains of the Mind* (2003), about wilderness and the Western imagination, won the Somerset Maugham Award and the *Guardian* First Book Award, among other prizes.

THE PEREGRINE

J. A. BAKER

Introduction by
ROBERT MACFARLANE

NEW YORK REVIEW BOOKS

New York

This is a New York Review Book
Published by The New York Review of Books
207 East 32nd Street, New York, NY 10016
www.nyrb.com

Published by arrangement with HarperCollins Publishers, Inc.

Library of Congress Cataloging-in-Publication Data
Baker, J. A. (John Alec)
  The peregrine / by J. A. Baker ; introduction by Robert Macfarlane.
     p. cm. — (New York Review Books classics)
  Originally published: New York : Harper & Row, 1967.
  ISBN 1-59017-133-0 (pbk. : alk. paper)
  1. Peregrine falcon—England—Anecdotes. I. Title. II. Series.
  QL795.B57B35 2005
  598.9'6—dc22
                                    2004026521

ISBN 978-1-59017-133-2

Printed in the United States of America on acid-free paper.
20 19

CONTENTS

INTRODUCTION

The Peregrine is, unmistakably, a masterpiece of twentieth-century nonfiction. As an elegy for a landscape, it stands alongside Barry Lopez's *Arctic Dreams*. In its dredging of melancholy and beauty from the English countryside, it rates with W. G. Sebald's *The Rings of Saturn*. As a fusion of the spiritual and the elemental, it matches Peter Matthiessen's *The Snow Leopard*. And as an account of a human obsession with a creature, it is peerless. Introductions are supposed to sound the trumpets for their books, of course, but there is nothing ceremonial about these claims. They are simply the case.

The plot of *The Peregrine*—if a book this unconventional can be said to possess a plot—runs as follows. One autumn, two pairs of peregrines come to hunt over an area of coastal East Anglia—a mixed terrain of marshland, wood, field, river valleys, mudflats, estuary, and sea. For a reason which is never fully explained, the narrator becomes obsessed with the birds. From October to April, he tracks them daily, and watches as they wash, fly, kill, eat, and roost. "Autumn," as he puts it, "begins my season of hawk-hunting, spring ends it, and winter glitters between like the arch of Orion." The book records these months of chase in all their agitated, monomaniacal repetitiveness, and describes them in a style so intense and incantatory that the act of bird-watching becomes one of sacred ritual.

Everything that occurs in *The Peregrine* takes place within the borders of the peregrines' hunting ground. The story does not extend beyond this landscape. No cause is specified for the quest itself, no triggering detail. No other human character besides Baker is admitted. We are told nothing of Baker's life outside the field: we do not even know where he sleeps or what he eats. All of this information, we sense, is withheld not to provoke inquiry, but because it is irrelevant.

Irrelevant, for *The Peregrine* is not a book about watching a bird, it is a book about becoming a bird. Early on, Baker sets out his manifesto of pursuit:

> Wherever he goes, this winter, I will follow him. I will share the fear, and the exaltation, and the boredom, of the hunting life. I will follow him till my predatory human shape no longer darkens in terror the shaken kaleidoscope of colour that stains the deep fovea of his brilliant eye. My pagan head shall sink into the winter land, and there be purified.

There, in four strange sentences, is the book's dramatic core. Baker hopes that, through a fierce, prolonged, and "purified" concentration upon the peregrine, he will somehow be able to escape his human form and abscond into the "brilliant" wildness of the bird.

As the seasons proceed, the narrator's relationship with the bird intensifies. He starts by learning to track the hawks. Peregrines can often fly so fast, and at such an altitude, that to the human eye they are invisible from the ground. But Baker discovers that the peregrines can be located by the disturbance they create among other birds, in the same way that the position of an invisible plane can be told from its contrail: "Evanescent as flame," he writes on October 7, "peregrines sear across the cold sky and are gone, leaving no sign in the blue haze above. But in the lower air a wake of birds trails back, and rises upward through the white helix of the gulls."

As he acquires his tracking skills, so Baker draws closer to the bird. One November day, he rests his hand on the grass where a peregrine has recently stood, and experiences "a strong feeling of proximity, identification." By the end of the month, he has turned fully feral. Crossing a field one afternoon, he sees feathers blowing in the wind:

> The body of a woodpigeon lay breast upward on a mass of soft white feathers. The head had been eaten.... The bones were still dark red, the blood still wet.
>
> I found myself crouching over the kill, like a mantling hawk. My eyes turned quickly about, alert for the walking heads of men. Unconsciously I was imitating the movements of a hawk, as in some primitive ritual; the hunter becoming the thing he hunts.... We live, in these days in the open, the same ecstatic fearful life. We shun men.

The pronouns tell the story—"I" turns into "we," human dissolves into hawk.

Of J. A. Baker himself, it is unnecessary to know much, nor is there much to know. Perhaps the only biographical detail worth noting is that he wrote *The Peregrine* following the diagnosis of a serious illness. This is never declared outright in the book, but it is nevertheless made clear that the narrator is suffering from some deep wound, mental or physical, which tinges his perception with "dimness" and "desolation," as well as sharpening his awareness of beauty.

The fact of Baker's illness explains the central drama of "the hunter becoming the things he hunts." For to abolish yourself through intense focus on another creature is, in a way, to evade death. It is an act of self-destruction which leads to resurrection. One thinks here of Keats's famous doctrine of "negative capability," the "poetical" capacity to empty yourself so totally into another being that you do not merely think like that being, but *are* that being. Keats's meditations on this subject were prompted in him by the sight of a bird. "If a sparrow come before my window," he wrote in November 1817, "I take part in its existence and pick about the gravel...[so] that I am in a very little time annihilated." This self-obliteration was precisely what Baker sought.

It is not only Baker who is under a possible sentence of death in *The Peregrine*, however. The hawks themselves are also menaced. The book was first published in 1967. In 1962, Rachel Carson had alerted the world to the murderous effects of pesticides on bird populations in her book *Silent Spring*. A year later, a British raptor specialist, Derek Ratcliffe, had written a landmark paper revealing the terrible impact of agrichemicals upon peregrine numbers in Britain.[1] In 1939 there were seven hundred pairs of peregrines in Britain; a 1962 survey showed a decline to 50 percent of this number, with only sixty-eight pairs appearing to have reared chicks successfully.

The mid-1960s, when Baker was writing his book, were a bleak time for the peregrine in Britain. It must have seemed

---

1. D. A. Ratcliffe, "The Status of the Peregrine in Great Britain," in *Bird Study*, Vol. 10 (1963), pp. 56–90. Ratcliffe's paper resulted in a control of DDT use in British agriculture, and the peregrine population saw a slow climb back up. By 1979, about two thirds of eyries were in use. In countries where pesticide use was not controlled the results were close to genocidal: 2000 pairs in Finland in 1950 had been reduced to sixteen pairs by 1975.

plausible to Baker—indeed it must have seemed likely—that the peregrine would become extinct, due to what he calls "the filthy, insidious pollen of farm chemicals." Baker had read Ratcliffe's paper; he had also seen firsthand the reduction of peregrine numbers. "Few winter in England now, fewer nest here," he mourns, "the ancient eyries are dying."

For the most part, an atmosphere of requiem prevails in *The Peregrine*: a soft sadness that things should be this way, mixed with a disbelief that they might be changed. Only once does this elegiac tone flare into anger. Out walking on December 24, a day of cusps and little light, Baker finds a heron, nearly dead, lying in a stubble field. Its wings are frozen to the ground, but in a ghastly thwarted mime of escape, it tries to fly off:

> As I approached I could see its whole body craving into flight. But it could not fly. I gave it peace, and saw the agonised sunlight of its eyes slowly heal with cloud.
>
> No pain, no death, is more terrible to a wild creature than its fear of man. . . . A poisoned crow, gaping and helplessly floundering in the grass, bright yellow foam bubbling from its throat, will dash itself up again and again on to the descending wall of air, if you try to catch it. A rabbit, inflated and foul with myxomatosis, . . . will feel the vibration of your footstep and will look for you with bulging, sightless eyes. . . .
>
> We are the killers. We stink of death. We carry it with us. It sticks to us like frost. We cannot tear it away.

"We stink of death. We carry it with us." By this point in the book, we understand that these are the words of a man who is himself deeply wounded and craving "peace"—but also the words of a man who is appalled to belong to his own species.

The Peregrine is a book in which very little happens, over and over again. Dawn. The man watches, the bird hunts, the bird kills, the bird feeds. Dusk. And so on, through seven months. For all its high-flown stylistic artifice, Baker's prose is grounded in everyday detail: in exact observations about the hunting habits of raptors, the flight patterns of starlings, terns, and seagulls, and the changing colors of trees and fields.

What Baker understood was that in order to keep the reader reading through the same cycle of events, he had to forge a new language of description. The language which he created was as instinctive, sudden, and aerial as the bird to which it was devoted, and one which, like the bird, could startle even as it repeated itself.

Again and again, Baker astonishes us at the level of the sentence. There are the neologisms: nouns sprung into verbs, and verbs torqued into adjectives. "Five thousand dunlin . . . rained away inland, like a horde of beetles gleamed with golden chitin." "The north wind brittled icily in the pleached lattice of the hedges." "Four short-eared owls soothed out of the gorse." There are the inversions— "Savagely he lashed himself free, and came superbly to the south, rising on the bright rim of the black cloud"; "Very still the estuary; misty skylines merged into white water"— which act as bugle notes, conferring a bright ritualism upon a scene. And there are the stunning set-piece descriptions, as formal and dynamic as any Imagist poem, of the chase and the "stoop": that "sabring fall from the sky," when the peregrine drops into its prey from a height of up to three thousand feet, killing with the shock of impact as much as with the slash of talons:

A falcon peregrine, sable on a white shield of sky, circled over from the sea. She slowed, and drifted aimlessly, as though the air above the land was thick and heavy. She dropped. The beaches flared and roared with salvoes of white wings. The sky shredded up, was torn by whirling birds. The falcon rose and fell, like a black billhook in splinters of white wood.

"The sky shredded up..." In Baker's hands, spaces and shapes, as well as words, behave unexpectedly towards one another. When a peregrine dives upon a "cumulus" of woodpigeons, "one bird fell back, gashed dead, looking astonished, like a man falling out of a tree. The ground came up and crushed it." Similarly, when a falcon chases and catches a dunlin, "the dunlin seemed to come slowly back to the hawk. It passed into his dark outline, and did not reappear." There is something curiously voluntary to the way the dunlin dies. With a little jolt, we realize that it is a moment which stands for the book itself: another sort of suicide, another slow merging with the hawk.

"What does a falcon see?" asked Anaximander of Miletus in the sixth century BC. According to Baker, a falcon sees like a Cubist painter. It perceives in planes and shapes, which slant abstractly towards one another. It remembers not detail but form and the interrelation of form:

The peregrine lives in a pouring-away world of no attachment, a world of wakes and tilting, of sinking planes of land and water. The peregrine sees and remembers patterns we do not know exist: the neat squares of orchard and woodland, the endlessly varying quadrilateral shapes of fields. He finds his way across the land by a succession of remembered symmetries.... He sees maps of black and white.

One of the many exhilarations of reading *The Peregrine* is
that we acquire the vision of a hawk. We gaze upon the East
Anglian landscape from above, and we see it as pure form:
partridges are "rings of small black stones" upon the fields,
lapwings hide in the "shiny corrugations" of a ploughed
field, an orchard shrinks "into dark twiggy lines and green
strips," the horizon is "stained with distant towns," an estuary "lifts up its blue and silver mouth." These are things we
would not have seen at ground level. We are blessed with
the sight of what the Greeks called the *katascopos*, the
"looker-down"—a view usually reserved for gods, birds, and
mountaineers. And how wonderfully unfamiliar it is to be
able to look down on Essex—a county which never rises
higher than 140 meters above sea level, a county which one
sees across or through, but rarely onto or upon.

The quality of deep strangeness with which Baker invests
the landscape is, to my mind, one of his most remarkable
achievements in *The Peregrine*. Any writer who makes the
English landscape his subject faces the problem of precedent. Each acre has been written about before. There is, it
can seem, nothing original, nothing primary, to find again.
An aspic layer of cliché clings and trembles over the land.
And yet Baker's Essex—fifty miles from London, heavily
farmed, densely peopled—is somehow made as mysterious,
elemental, wild, and remote as anywhere in the world.

One way Baker effects this is to avoid official place-
names. Instead he names his own place into being. He
speaks of "the South," "the North," "the East," and "the
West." He inhabits a cardinal landscape. When he is traveling, he steers himself only by landform and feature, heading
"inland," "up the slope of the hill," "along the line of the

woods." Baker also miraculously depopulates his countryside. The odd walker is seen, ships move out at sea, a red tractor combs a field. Otherwise, an eerie emptiness prevails. This is, of course, because Baker is avoiding "humans," of whom he does not wish to count himself one. He has gone wild, and keeps to the hedges, the trees, and the shadows, as both the hunter and the hunted must always do.

Everything contained within *The Peregrine*—the landscape, the narrator, the birds, the language—behaves in unpredictable ways. Everything is surprised into strange and beautiful expression by the passage of the hawk and the sweep of the narrator's hawklike gaze. This is a book which sets the imagination aloft, and keeps it there for months and years afterwards.

—ROBERT MACFARLANE

THE PEREGRINE

To My Wife

Part 1

BEGINNINGS

Part 1

BEGINNINGS

East of my home, the long ridge lies across the skyline like the low hull of a submarine. Above it, the eastern sky is bright with reflections of distant water, and there is a feeling of sails beyond land. Hill trees mass together in a dark-spired forest, but when I move towards them they slowly fan apart, the sky descends between, and they are solitary oaks and elms, each with its own wide territory of winter shadow. The calmness, the solitude of horizons lures me towards them, through them, and on to others. They layer the memory like strata.

From the town, the river flows north-east, bends east round the north side of the ridge, turns south to the estuary. The upper valley is a flat open plain, lower down it is narrow and steep-sided, near the estuary it is again flat and open. The plain is like an estuary of land, scattered with island farms. The river flows slowly, meanders; it is too small for the long, wide estuary, which was once the mouth of a much larger river that drained most of middle England.

Detailed descriptions of landscape are tedious. One part of England is superficially so much like another. The differences are subtle, coloured by love. The soil here is clay: boulder clay to the north of the river, London clay to the south. There is gravel on the river terraces, and on the higher ground of the ridge. Once forest, then pasture, the land is now mainly arable. Woods are small, with few large trees; chiefly oak standards with hornbeam or hazel coppice. Many hedges have been cut down. Those that still stand are of hawthorn, blackthorn, and elm. Elms grow tall in the clay; their varying shapes contour the winter sky. Cricket-bat willows mark the river's course, alders line the brook. Hawthorn grows well. It is a country of elm and oak and thorn. People native to the clay are surly and slow to burn, morose and smouldering as alder wood, laconic, heavy as the land itself.

There are four hundred miles of tidal coast, if all the creeks and islands are included; it is the longest and most irregular county coastline. It is the driest county, yet watery-edged, flaking down to marsh and salting and mud-flat. The drying sandy mud of the ebb-tide makes the sky clear above; clouds reflect water and shine it back inland.

Farms are well ordered, prosperous, but a fragrance of neglect still lingers, like a ghost of fallen grass. There is always a sense of loss, a feeling of being forgotten. There is nothing else here; no castles, no ancient monuments, no hills like green clouds. It is just a curve of the earth, a rawness of winter fields. Dim, flat, desolate lands that cauterise all sorrow.

I have always longed to be a part of the outward life, to be out there at the edge of things, to let the human taint wash away in emptiness and silence as the fox sloughs his smell into the cold unworldliness of water; to return to the town as a stranger. Wandering flushes a glory that fades with arrival.

I came late to the love of birds. For years I saw them only as a tremor at the edge of vision. They know suffering and joy in simple states not possible for us. Their lives quicken and warm to a pulse our hearts can never reach. They race to oblivion. They are old before we have finished growing.

The first bird I searched for was the nightjar, which used to nest in the valley. Its song is like the sound of a stream of wine spilling from a height into a deep and booming cask. It is an odorous sound, with a bouquet that rises to the quiet sky. In the glare of day it would seem thinner and drier, but dusk mellows it and gives it vintage. If a song could smell, this song would smell of crushed grapes and almonds and dark wood. The sound spills out, and none of it is lost. The whole wood brims with it. Then it stops. Suddenly, unexpectedly. But the ear hears it still, a prolonged and fading echo, draining and winding out among the surrounding trees. Into the deep stillness, between the early stars and the long afterglow, the nightjar leaps up joyfully. It glides and flutters, dances and bounces, lightly, silently away. In pictures it seems to have a frog-like despondency, a mournful aura, as though it were sepulchred in twilight, ghostly and disturbing. It is never like that in life. Through the dusk, one sees only its shape and its flight, intangibly light and gay, graceful and nimble as a swallow.

Sparrowhawks were always near me in the dusk, like something I meant to say but could never quite remember. Their narrow heads glared blindly through my sleep. I pursued them for many summers, but they were hard to find and harder to see, being so few and so wary. They lived a fugitive, guerrilla life. In all the overgrown neglected places the frail bones of generations of sparrowhawks are sifting down now into the deep humus of the woods. They were a banished race of beautiful barbarians, and when they died they could not be replaced.

I have turned away from the musky opulence of the summer woods, where so many birds are dying. Autumn begins my season of hawk-hunting, spring ends it, winter glitters between like the arch of Orion.

I saw my first peregrine on a December day at the estuary ten years ago. The sun reddened out of the white river mist, fields glittered with rime, boats were encrusted with it; only the gently lapping water moved freely and shone. I went along the high river-wall towards the sea. The stiff crackling white grass became limp and wet as the sun rose through a clear sky into dazzling mist. Frost stayed all day in shaded places, the sun was warm, there was no wind.

I rested at the foot of the wall and watched dunlin feeding at the tide-line. Suddenly they flew upstream, and hundreds of finches fluttered overhead, whirling away with a 'hurr' of desperate wings. Too slowly it came to me that something was happening which I ought not to miss. I scrambled up, and saw that the stunted hawthorns on the inland slope of the wall were full of fieldfares. Their sharp bills pointed to the north-east, and they clacked and spluttered in alarm. I followed their point, and saw a falcon flying towards me. It veered to the right , and passed inland. It was like a kestrel, but bigger and yellower, with a more bullet-shaped head, longer wings, and greater zest and buoyancy of flight. It did not glide till it saw starlings feeding in stubble, then it swept down and was hidden among them as they rose. A minute later it rushed overhead and was gone in a breath into the sunlit mist. It was flying much higher than before, flinging and darting forwards, with its sharp wings angled back and flicking like a snipe's.

This was my first peregrine. I have seen many since then, but none has excelled it for speed and fire of spirit. For ten years I spent all my winters searching for that restless brilliance, for the sudden passion and violence that peregrines flush from the sky. For ten years I have been looking upward for that cloud-biting anchor shape, that crossbow flinging through the air. The eye becomes insatiable for hawks. It clicks towards them with ecstatic fury, just as the hawk's eye swings and dilates to the luring food-shapes of gulls and pigeons.

To be recognised and accepted by a peregrine you must wear the same clothes, travel by the same way, perform actions in the same order. Like all birds, it fears the unpredictable. Enter and leave the same fields at the same time each day, soothe the hawk from its wildness by a ritual of behaviour as invariable as its own. Hood the glare of the eyes, hide the white tremor of the hands, shade the stark reflecting face, assume the stillness of a tree. A peregrine fears nothing he can see clearly and far off. Approach him across open ground with a steady unfaltering movement. Let your shape grow in size but do not alter its outline. Never hide yourself unless concealment is complete. Be alone. Shun the furtive oddity of man, cringe from the hostile eyes of farms. Learn to fear. To share fear is the greatest bond of all. The hunter must become the thing he hunts. What is, is now, must have the quivering intensity of an arrow thudding into a tree. Yesterday is dim and monochrome. A week ago you were not born. Persist, endure, follow, watch.

Hawk-hunting sharpens vision. Pouring away behind the moving bird, the land flows out from the eye in deltas of piercing colour. The angled eye strikes through the surface dross as the obliqued axe cuts to the heart of a tree. A vivid sense of place grows like another limb. Direction has colour and meaning. South is a bright, blocked place, opaque and stifling; West is a thickening of the earth into trees, a drawing together, the great beef side of England, the heavenly haunch; North is open, bleak, a way to nothing; East is a quickening in the sky, a beckoning of light, a storming suddenness of sea. Time is measured by a clock of blood. When one is active, close to the hawk, pursuing, the pulse races, time goes faster; when one is still, waiting, the pulse quietens, time is slow. Always, as one hunts for the hawk, one has an oppressive sense of time contracting inwards like a tightening spring. One hates the movement of the sun, the steady alteration of the light, the increase of hunger, the maddening metronome of the heart-beat. When one says 'ten o'clock' or 'three o'clock,' this is not the grey and shrunken time of towns; it is the memory of a certain fulmination or declension of light that was unique to that time and that place on that day, a memory as vivid to the hunter as burning magnesium. As soon as the hawk-hunter steps from his door he knows the way of the wind, he feels the weight of the air. Far within himself he seems to see the hawk's day growing steadily towards the light of their first encounter. Time and the weather hold both hawk and watcher between their turning poles. When the hawk is found, the hunter can look lovingly back at all the tedium and misery of searching and waiting that went before. All is transfigured, as though the broken columns of a ruined temple had suddenly resumed their ancient splendour.

I shall try to make plain the bloodiness of killing. Too often this has been slurred over by those who defend hawks. Flesh-eating man is in no way superior. It is so easy to love the dead. The word 'predator' is baggy with misuse. All birds eat living flesh at some time in their lives. Consider the cold-eyed thrush, that springy carnivore of lawns, worm stabber, basher to death of snails. We should not sentimentalise his song, and forget the killing that sustains it.

In my diary of a single winter I have tried to preserve a unity, binding together the bird, the watcher, and the place that holds them both. Everything I describe took place while I was watching it, but I do not believe that honest observation is enough. The emotions and behaviour of the watcher are also facts, and they must be truthfully recorded.

For ten years I followed the peregrine. I was possessed by it. It was a grail to me. Now it has gone. The long pursuit is over. Few peregrines are left, there will be fewer, they may not survive. Many die on their backs, clutching insanely at the sky in their last convulsions, withered and burnt away by the filthy, insidious pollen of farm chemicals. Before it is too late, I have tried to recapture the extraordinary beauty of this bird and to convey the wonder of the land he lived in, a land to me as profuse and glorious as Africa. It is a dying world, like Mars, but glowing still.

EDITOR'S NOTE FOR THE AMERICAN EDITION

Many of the birds described in this book are "old world" and therefore unfamiliar to Americans. The *fieldfare* is a robin-like thrush; the *nightjar* resembles our whip-poor-will; the *jackdaw* and *rook* are crows. The *moorhen* is a common gallinule. The *lapwing* and *redshank* are shorebirds: the former is a crested plover; the latter is very much like our yellowlegs (but with red legs). The *woodpigeon* is a large, wild pigeon; the *chaffinch* and *bullfinch* are European songbirds (the latter is related to the pine grosbeak). The *pipistrelle* is a bat.

The peregrine is the most awe-inspiring bird in American Skies. In both the United States and England it is losing ground to civilization - chiefly because of man's use of pesticides.

Part 2

PEREGRINES

Part 2

PEREGRINES

The hardest thing of all to see is what is really there. Books about birds show pictures of the peregrine, and the text is full of information. Large and isolated in the gleaming whiteness of the page, the hawk stares back at you, bold, statuesque, brightly coloured. But when you have shut the book, you will never see that bird again. Compared with the close and static image, the reality will seem dull and disappointing. The living bird will never be so large, so shiny-bright. It will be deep in landscape, and always sinking farther back, always at the point of being lost. Pictures are waxworks beside the passionate mobility of the living bird.

Female peregrines, known as falcons, are between seventeen and twenty inches long; roughly the length of a man's arm from elbow to fingertip. Males, or tiercels, are three to four inches shorter, fourteen to sixteen inches long. Weights also vary: falcons from $1\frac{3}{4}$ to $2\frac{1}{2}$ pounds, tiercels from $1\frac{1}{4}$ to $1\frac{3}{4}$ pounds. Everything about peregrines varies: colour, size, weight, personality, style: everything.

Adults are blue, blue-black, or grey, above; whitish below, barred crosswise with grey. During their first year of life, and often for much of their second year also, the younger birds are brown above, and buff below—streaked vertically with brown. This brown colour ranges from foxy red to sepia, the buff from pale cream to pale yellow. Peregrines are born between April and June. They do not begin to moult their juvenile feathers till the following March; many do not begin till they are more than a year old. Some may remain in brown plumage throughout their second winter, though they usually begin to show some adult feathers from January onwards. The moult may take as long as six months to complete. Warmth speeds it, cold retards it. Peregrines do not breed till they are two years old, but one-year birds may select an eyrie and defend territory.

The peregrine is adapted to the pursuit and killing of birds in flight. Its shape is streamlined. The rounded head and wide chest taper smoothly back to the narrow wedge-shaped tail. The wings are long and pointed; the primaries long and slender for speed, the secondaries long and broad to give strength for the lifting and carrying of heavy prey. The hooked bill can pull flesh from bones. It has a tooth on the upper mandible, which fits into a notch in the lower one. This tooth can be inserted between the neck vertebrae of a bird so that, by pressing and twisting, the peregrine is able to snap the spinal cord. The legs are thick and muscular, the toes long and powerful. The toes have bumpy pads on their undersides that help in the gripping of prey. The bird-killing hind toe is the longest of the four, and it can be used separately for striking prey to the ground. The huge pectoral muscles give power and endurance in flight. The dark feathering around the eyes absorbs light and reduces glare. The contrasting facial pattern of brown and white may also have the effect of startling prey into sudden flight. To some extent it also camouflages the large, light-reflecting eyes.

The speed of the peregrine's wing-beat has been recorded as 4.4 beats per second. Comparative figures are: jackdaw 4.3, crow 4.2, lapwing 4.8, woodpigeon 5.2. In level flapping flight the peregrine looks rather pigeon-like, but its wings are longer and more flexible than a pigeon's and they curl higher above the back. The typical flight has been described as a succession of quick wing-beats, broken at regular intervals by long glides with wings extended. In fact, gliding is far from regular, and at least half the peregrine flights I have seen have contained few, if any, glides. When the hawk is not hunting, the flight may seem slow and undulating, but it is always faster than it looks. I have timed it at between thirty and forty miles an hour, and it is seldom less than that. Level pursuit of prey has reached speeds of fifty to sixty miles an hour over distances of a mile or more; speeds in excess of sixty m.p.h. were only attained for a much shorter time. The speed of the vertical stoop is undoubtedly well over a hundred miles an hour, but it is impossible to be more precise. The excitement of seeing a peregrine stoop cannot be defined by the use of statistics.

Peregrines arrive on the east coast from mid-August to November; the majority reach here in late September and the first half of October. They may come in from the sea in any weather conditions, but are most likely to do so on a clear sunny day with a fresh north-west wind blowing. Passage birds may stay in one area for two to three weeks before going south. Return passage lasts from late February to May. Winter residents usually depart in late March or early April. Juvenile falcons are the first peregrines to arrive in the autumn, followed by juvenile tiercels, and later by a few adult birds. Most adults do not come so far south, but remain as close as they can to their breeding territory. This order of migration, which prevails along the European coastline from the North Cape to Brittany, is similar to that observed on the eastern coast of North America. Ringing recoveries suggest that immigrants to the east coast of England have come from Scandinavia. No British-ringed peregrines have been recovered in south-east England. Generally speaking, all the juveniles that wintered in the river valley, and along the estuaries, were paler in colour than juveniles from British nests; they had a distinctive wing pattern of light reddish-brown wing coverts and secondaries contrasting with black primaries, similar to that of a kestrel.

The territory in which my observations were made measures roughly twenty miles from east to west and ten miles from north to south. It was hunted over by at least two peregrines each winter, sometimes by three or four. The river valley and the estuary to the east of it are both ten miles in length. Together they formed a long narrow centre to the territory, where at least one peregrine could always be found. Why these particular places were chosen it is difficult to be sure. Most parts of England, including towns and cities, could provide a winter's keep for a resident peregrine, yet certain areas have always been regularly visited, while others have been ignored. Peregrines that have a definite liking for duck or shore birds will obviously be found on the coast, at reservoirs and sewage farms, or in fenland. But the birds that wintered in the valley took a wide range of prey, in which woodpigeons and black-headed gulls predominated. I think they came here for two reasons: because this was a wintering place that had been used for many years, and because the gravelly streams of the valley provided ideal conditions for bathing. The peregrine is devoted to tradition. The same nesting cliffs are occupied for hundreds of years. It is probable that the same wintering territories are similarly occupied by each generation of juvenile birds. They may in fact be returning to places where their ancestors nested. Peregrines that now nest in the tundra conditions of Lapland and the Norwegian mountains may be the descendants of those birds that once nested in the tundra regions of the lower Thames. Peregrines have always lived as near the permafrost limit as possible.

Peregrines bathe every day. They prefer running water, six to nine inches deep; nothing less than two inches or more than twelve inches is acceptable to them. The bed of the stream must be stony and firm, with a shallow incline sloping gradually down from the bank. They favour those places where the colour of the stream-bed resembles the colour of their own plumage. They like to be concealed by steep banks or overhanging bushes. Shallow streams, brooks, or deep ditches, are preferred to rivers. Salt water is seldom used. Dykes lined with concrete are sometimes chosen, but only if the concrete has been discoloured. Shallow fords, where brown-mottled country lanes are crossed by a fast-running brook, are favourite places. For warning of human approach they rely on their remarkably keen hearing and on the alarm calls of other birds. The search for a suitable bathing place is one of the peregrine's main daily activities, and their hunting and roosting places are located in relation to this search. They bathe frequently to rid themselves of their own feather lice and of the lice that may transfer to them from the prey they have killed. These new lice are unlikely to live long once they have left their natural host species, but they are an additional irritation to which the hawk is most sensitive. Unless the number of lice infesting the hawk's feathers is controlled by regular bathing, there can be a rapid deterioration in health, which is dangerous for a juvenile bird still learning to hunt and kill its prey.

Though there can be many variations, a peregrine's day usually begins with a slow, leisurely flight from the roosting place to the nearest suitable bathing stream. This may be as much as ten to fifteen miles away. After bathing, another hour or two is spent in drying the feathers, preening ,and sleeping. The hawk rouses only gradually from his post-bathing lethargy. His first flights are short and unhurried. He moves from perch to perch, watching other birds and occasionally catching an insect or a mouse on the ground. He re-enacts the whole process of learning to kill that he went through when he first left the eyrie: the first, short, tentative flights; the longer, more confident ones; the playful, mock attacks at inanimate objects, such as falling leaves or drifting feathers; the games with other birds, changing to a pretence of attack, and then to the first serious attempt to kill. True hunting may be a comparatively brief process at the end of this long re-enactment of the hawk's adolescence.

Hunting is always preceded by some form of play. The hawk may feint at partridges, harass jackdaws or lapwings, skirmish with crows. Sometimes, without warning, he will suddenly kill. Afterwards he seems baffled by what he has done, and he may leave the kill where it fell and return to it later when he is genuinely hunting. Even when he is hungry, and has killed in anger, he may sit beside his prey for ten to fifteen minutes before starting to feed. In these cases the dead bird is usually unmarked, and the hawk seems to be puzzled by it. He nudges it idly with his bill. When blood flows, he feeds at once.

Regular hunting over the same area will produce an increasingly effective defensive reaction from possible prey. It is always noticeable that the reaction of birds to a peregrine flying above them is comparatively slight in September and October, but that it steadily increases throughout the winter, till in March it is violent and spectacular. The peregrine has to avoid frightening the same birds too often, or they may leave the area altogether. For this reason he may be seen hunting in the same place for several days in succession, and then not be seen there again for a week or more. He may move only a short distance, or he may go twenty miles away. Individuals vary greatly in their hunting habits. Some hunt across their territory in straight lines five to fifteen miles long. They may suddenly turn about and fly back on the same course to attack birds already made uneasy. These hunting lines may run from estuary to reservoir, from reservoir to valley, and from valley to estuary; or they may follow the lines of flight from roosting places to bathing places. The territory is also effectively quartered by long up-wind flights, followed by diagonal down and cross wind gliding that finishes a mile or two away from the original starting point. Hunting on sunny days is done chiefly by soaring and circling down wind, and is based on a similar diagonal quartering of the ground. When an attack is made, it is usually a single vicious stoop. If it misses, the hawk may fly on at once to look for other prey.

In early autumn, and in spring, when days are longer and the air warmer, the peregrine soars higher and hunts over a wider area. In March, when conditions are often ideal for soaring, his range increases, and by long stoops from a great height he is able to kill larger and heavier prey, Cloudy weather means shorter flights at lower levels. Rain curtails the hunting range still further. Fog reduces it to a single field. The shorter the day the more active the hawk, for there is less time available for hunting. All its activities contract or expand with the shortening or lengthening of days on either side of the winter solstice.

Juvenile peregrines hover whenever the wind is too strong to allow them to circle sufficiently slowly above the area they are surveying. Such hovering usually lasts for ten to twenty seconds, but some birds are more addicted to the habit than others and will hover persistently for long periods. The hunting hawk uses every advantage he can. Height is the obvious one. He may stoop (stoop is another word for swoop) at prey from any height between three feet and three thousand. Ideally, prey is taken by surprise: by a hawk hidden by height and diving unseen to his victim, or by a hawk that rushes suddenly out from concealment in a tree or a dyke. Like a sparrowhawk, the peregrine will wait in ambush. The more spectacular methods of killing are used less often by juveniles than they are by adults. Some soaring peregrines deliberately stoop with the sun behind them. They do it too frequently for it to be merely a matter of chance.

Like all hunters, the peregrine is inhibited by a code of behaviour. It seldom chases prey on the ground or pursues it into cover, in the manner of other hawks, though it is quite capable of doing so. Many adults take only birds in flight, but juveniles are less particular. Peregrines perfect their killing power by endless practice, like knights or sportsmen. Those most adaptable, within the limits of the code, survive. If the code is persistently broken, the hawk is probably sick or insane.

Killing is simple once the peregrine has the advantage of his prey. Small, light birds are seized in his outstretched foot; larger, heavier birds are stooped at from above, at any angle between ten and ninety degrees, and are often struck to the ground. The stoop is a means of increasing the speed at which the hawk makes contact with his prey. The momentum of the stoop adds weight to the hawk and enables him to kill birds twice as heavy as himself. Young peregrines have to be taught to stoop by their parents; captive birds have to be trained by falconers in a similar way. The action of stopping does not seem to be innate, though it is quickly learnt. The ability to stoop at birds in flight was probably a comparatively recent evolutionary development, superseding capture by follow-chase and the taking of ground-game. Most birds still fly up from the ground when a peregrine passes above them, though this may increase their vulnerability.

The peregrine swoops down towards his prey. As he descends, his legs are extended forward till the feet are underneath his breast. The toes are clenched, with the long hind toe projecting below the three front ones, which are bent up out of the way. He passes close to the bird, almost touching it with his body, and still moving very fast. His extended hind toe (or toes—sometimes one, sometimes both) gashes into the back or breast of the bird, like a knife. At the moment of impact the hawk raises his wings above his back. If the prey is cleanly hit—and it is usually hit hard or missed altogether—it dies at once, either from shock or from the perforation of some vital organ. A peregrine weights between 1½ and 2½ lbs.; such a weight, falling from a hundred feet, will kill all but the largest birds. Shelduck, pheasants, or great black-backed gulls, usually succumb to a stoop of five hundred feet or more. Sometimes the prey is seized and then released, so that it tumbles to the ground, stunned but still alive; or it may be clutched and carried off to a suitable feeding place. The hawk breaks its neck with his bill, either while he is carrying it or immediately he alights. No flesh-eating creature is more efficient, or more merciful, than the peregrine. It is not deliberately merciful; it simply does what it was designed to do. The crow-catchers of Königsberg kill their prey in the same way. Having decoyed the crows into their nets, they kill them by biting them in the neck, severing the spinal cord with their teeth.

The peregrine plucks feathers from his prey before he begins to eat. The amount of plucking varies, not only with the hunger of the hawk, but also according to individual preference. Some hawks always pluck their prey thoroughly, others pull out only a few beakfuls of feathers. Peregrines hold the prey steady by standing on it, gripping it with the inner talon of one or both feet. Plucking takes two to three minutes. Eating takes ten minutes to half an hour, depending on the size of the prey; ten minutes for a fieldfare or redshank, half an hour for a pheasant or mallard.

Prey may be eaten where it falls, if it is too heavy to carry off, or if it has landed in a suitable place. Many peregrines seem to be quite indifferent, feeding wherever they happen to make a kill. Others prefer a completely open place, or a completely secluded one. Seventy per cent of the kills I have found were lying on short grass, although most of the land here is arable. Peregrines like a firm surface to feed on. Small kills are often

27

eaten in trees, especially in autumn. Birds reared in tree nests may eat their kills in trees whenever possible. On the coast, some peregrines prefer the top of the sea-wall for feeding, others eat at the foot of the wall, near the water line. The latter may have come from cliff eyries and be used to a steep slope above them as they eat.

A peregrine kill can be easily recognised. The framework of a bird is left on its back, with the wings untouched and still attached to the body by the shoulder-girdles. The breast-bone and all the main bones of the body may be quite flesh-less. If the head has been left, the neck vertebrae will usually be fleshless also. The legs and back are frequently left untouched. If the breast-bone is still intact, small triangular pieces will have been nipped out of it by the peregrine's bill. (This is not always true of very large birds, which have thicker bones.) When a kill is left with a good deal of meat still on it, the peregrine may return next day, or even several days later, to finish it up. Surplus meat from abandoned kills helps to support foxes, rats, stoats, weasels, crows, kestrels, gulls, tramps, and gypsies. The feathers are used by long-tailed tits in the construction of their nests. I have found an unusual concentration of such nests in areas where many kills have been made.

No other predator conflicts with the peregrine in the pursuit of prey, but it is sometimes prevented from hunting in certain places by the determined and concerted attacks of crows. When man is hunting, the peregrine goes elsewhere. It is remarkably quick to distinguish between an unarmed man and a man with a gun. There is a curious relationship between peregrines and kestrels that is difficult to define. The two species are often seen in the same place, especially in autumn and spring. I rarely saw one of them without finding the other close by. They may share the same bathing places, the peregrine may occasionally rob the kestrel of its prey, the kestrel may feed on kills the peregrine has left, the peregrine may attack birds that the kestrel unwittingly puts up for him. In September and October some peregrines seem to copy the kestrel's way of hunting, and I have seen the two species hovering together over the same field. In a similar way, I have seen a peregrine hunting near a short-eared owl, and apparently mimicking its style of flight. By March the relationship between kestrel and peregrine has changed; the peregrine has become hostile, and will stoop at, and probably kill, any kestrel hovering near him.

During ten winters I found 619 peregrine kills. Individual species were represented as follows:

Woodpigeon	38%
Black-headed gull	14%
Lapwing	6%
Wigeon	3%
Partridge	3%
Fieldfare	3%
Moorhen	2%
Curlew	2%
Golden plover	2%
Rook	2%

In addition to these ten, there were 35 other species taken, to make up the remaining 25% of the total. Analysed by families, these are the proportions:

Pigeons	39%
Gulls	17%
Waders	16%
Duck	8%
Game	5%
Corvids	5%
Small or medium-sized Passerines	5%
Others	5%

More woodpigeons were killed during the winter I have described in this book, because of their extraordinary abundance in the cold weather, and because of the absence of other inland species at that time. The relative figures for this particular winter are as follows:

Woodpigeon	54%
Black-headed gull	9%
Lapwing	7%
Wigeon	3%
Partridge	3%
Fieldfare	2%
Moorhen	2%
Curlew	2%
Rook	2%
Mallard	2%

The remaining 14% was made up of 22 other species.

These tables suggest that the juvenile peregrine preys mainly on those species that are most numerous in its hunting territory, provided they weigh at least half a pound. Sparrows and starlings are very common here, but few are killed by peregrines. Of the larger birds, the commonest and most widely distributed species are woodpigeons, black-headed gulls, and lapwings, in that order. If the total weight of available prey is considered, the woodpigeon probably represents a proportion of the total biomass approximately equal to the percentage of woodpigeons actually killed by the peregrine. The method of selection employed, if there is one, may in fact be nothing more spectacular than this: that the peregrine kills most frequently the species of bird it sees most frequently, provided it is a reasonably large and conspicuous one. The presence of abnormally large numbers of any species of bird invariably results in a higher proportion of that species being killed by the peregrine. If a dry summer enables more partridges to breed successfully, then more partridges will be taken by the peregrine during the following winter. If wigeon numbers increase when the cold weather comes, more wigeon will be killed. Predators that kill what is commonest have the best chance of survival. Those that develop a preference for one species only are more likely to go hungry and to succumb to disease.

Over the valley and the estuary, many gulls and lapwings are killed by the peregrine in October and November, chiefly from freshly ploughed land. From December to February woodpigeons are the main prey, especially in hard weather, when fewer lapwings are available. Woodpigeons are still taken in March, the killing of lapwings and gulls increases again, and more duck are killed than in any other month. Game-birds, moorhens, fieldfares, and waders, are taken occasionally throughout the winter. In rain or fog, game-birds and moorhens become the principal prey. Ducks are killed far less often than is popularly supposed. This is true of all countries, both in summer and winter; the peregrine is definitely not a 'duck-hawk'. Domestic and feral pigeons figure highly in most lists of peregrine kills, but I have found none here. No peregrine I have seen has ever attacked them, or shown any interest in them at all.

The peregrine's choice of prey can be affected by weather conditions. When a wet summer is followed by a wet winter, the land becomes waterlogged, ploughing is delayed, and the valley bathing-places are covered by flood-water. Peregrines then hunt over the grasslands to the south of the valley and between the two estuaries. They bathe in ditches or at the edge of flood-water. Some birds prefer to hunt over grass-land, irrespective of weather conditions. These green-country peregrines arrive late in the autumn and stay till late April or early May. Possibly they come from the Lapland tundra, where the country, in summer, is like a huge emerald sponge. The wet marsh pastures, and the green fields of the heavy clay, are the colour of home to them. They range over vast distances, they fly high, they are much harder to find and follow than the comparatively sedentary peregrines of the valley. Lapwings, gulls, and fieldfares, feeding on worms in wet pastures, are their favourite prey. Clover-eating woodpigeons are taken from January to March. Nest-building rooks are often attacked.

It seems unlikely that the peregrine can have a discriminating sense of taste. If it has a preference for a certain species, it is probably because of the texture of the flesh and the amount of tender meat on the bones. Rooks, jackdaws, gulls, sawbill ducks and grebes, are all more or less distasteful to the human palate, but are eaten by the peregrine with apparent relish.

Conspicuousness of colour or pattern increases vulnerability and influences the peregrine's choice of prey. Birds moving from place to place are always vulnerable, whether they are flying to and from their roosts along known ways, or merely passing over the territory on migration. Recent arrivals are attacked at once, before they can learn refuges. The odd are always singled out. The albinos, the sick, the deformed, the solitary, the imbecile, the senile, the very young; these are the most vulnerable.

Predators overcome their prey by the exploitation of weakness rather than by superior power. As in the following instances:

Woodpigeon.

The white wing and neck feathers are visible at a great distance. White shows up against all ground-colours. The peregrine sees and reacts to white more rapidly than to any colour. Eighty per cent of the birds killed in the territory were either mainly white or showed conspicuous white markings. Woodpigeons are also betrayed by the loud clatter of their wings at take-off. In spring, their display flight makes them still more obvious. Their flocks gain height too slowly, and the individual birds do not keep close enough together. They are strong in level flight; they are quick to see danger from below and to swerve suddenly aside; but when attacked from above, their reaction is less violent, they dodge with difficulty, their straight flight is slow to bend. Because they are so much shot at and disturbed by man they are often forced to fly beneath the hunting hawk. They are loose-feathered and easy to pluck. In every respect they are an ideal species for the peregrine to prey upon. They are noisy, conspicuous, numerous, heavy, well-fleshed, nourishing, and not hard to kill.

Black-headed gull.

White gulls are the most conspicuous of all winter birds. Against dark ploughland they are visible even to the feeble human eye when half a mile away. That is why the peregrine kills so many adult gulls, and so few juveniles. Gulls can rise quickly to evade the stoop, but they are easily driven to panic by attack from below. Their whiteness blends with the sky. It may make them invisible to the fish they live on when at sea. Relying on camouflage, perhaps they are slow to adapt themselves to unexpected danger from beneath. It was once believed that peregrines detested gull-flesh. This is certainly not true of the birds that winter here, though inland feeding may take away the fishy taste from gull-flesh. Many gulls are killed by Finnish peregrines during the summer, and gulls are frequently taken on the coast of Norway, and in Scotland.

Lapwing

They are well hidden when feeding in a field, but the flocks always fly up when a peregrine goes over. As soon as they rise, their black and white tails are a target to the falcon's eye. Their spring display flight makes them careless of danger and less alert to predators. They have the reputation of being hard to kill, but the peregrines I have seen have outflown them fairly easily.

Wigeon.

Peregrines prefer wigeon to any other species of duck. It is the commonest coastal duck, in winter, and its broad white wing-markings and loud whistling calls make it very conspicuous. Like all duck, it flies fast and straight, but it cannot dodge easily from the stoop. In March the paired birds are slow to react to the peregrine's approach. When wildfowling finishes in February, the peregrine kills more duck and is often seen hunting on the coast at nightfall.

To summarise, these are the characteristics that make birds vulnerable to peregrine attack: white or light-coloured plumage or markings, too great a reliance on cryptic colouring, loud repetitive calling, audible wing-beats, straight inflexible flight, prolonged and high song-flight (e.g. skylark and redshank), display and fighting by males in spring, feeding too far from adequate refuge, the habitual use of the same feeding and bathing places, flying to and from roost along known ways, the failure of a flock to bunch together when attacked.

The quantity of food eaten by wild peregrines is difficult to estimate accurately. Captive peregrines are given four to five ounces of beef daily (or its equivalent). Wild juveniles probably eat more than this. A wild tiercel will kill and eat two lapwings each day, or two black-headed gulls, or one woodpigeon. A falcon may eat two woodpigeons—though not wholly—or one larger bird, such as a mallard or a curlew.

During March, a greater variety of prey is taken, including a wider range of bird species and a surprisingly large number of mammals. Moult is beginning, and the time for migration is near. An increased blood supply is needed for the growth of new feathers. The peregrine seems to be always eating. Two birds are killed daily, as well as mice, worms, and insects.

The eyes of a falcon peregrine weigh approximately one ounce each; they are larger and heavier than human eyes. If our eyes were in the same proportion to our bodies as the peregrine's are to his, a twelve stone man would have eyes three inches across, weighing four pounds. The whole retina of a hawk's eye records a resolution of distant objects that is twice as acute as that of the human retina. Where the lateral and binocular visions focus, there are deep-pitted foveal areas; their numerous cells record a resolution eight times as great as ours. This means that a hawk, endlessly scanning the landscape with small abrupt turns of his head, will pick up any point of movement; by focussing upon it he can immediately make it flare up into larger, clearer view.

The peregrine's view of the land is like the yachtsman's view of the shore as he sails into the long estuaries. A wake of water recedes behind him, the wake of the pierced horizon glides back on either side. Like the seafarer, the peregrine lives in a pouring-away world of no attachment, a world of wakes and tilting, of sinking planes of land and water. We who are anchored and earthbound cannot envisage this freedom of the eye. The peregrine sees and remembers patterns we do not know exist: the neat squares of orchard and woodland, the endlessly varying quadrilateral shapes of fields. He finds his way across the land by a succession of remembered symmetries. But what does he understand? Does he really 'know' that an object that increases in size is moving towards him? Or is it that he believes in the size he sees, so that a distant man is too small to be frightening but a man near is a man huge and therefore terrifying? He may live in a world of endless pulsations, of objects forever contracting or dilating in size. Aimed at a distant bird, a flutter of white wings, he may feel—as it spreads out beneath him like a stain of white—that he can never fail to strike. Everything he is has been evolved to link the targeting eye to the striking talon.

Part 3

THE HUNTING LIFE

Part 3

THE HUNTING LIFE

October 1st. Autumn rises into the bright sky. Corn is down. Fields shine after harvest.

Over orchards smelling of vinegary windfalls, busy with tits and bullfinches, a peregrine glides to perch in a river-bank alder. River shadows ripple on the spare, haunted face of the hawk in the water. They cross the cold eyes of the watching heron. Sunlight glints. The heron blinds the white river cornea with the spear of his bill. The hawk flies quickly upward to the breaking clouds.

Swerving and twisting away from the misty lower air, he rises to the first faint warmth of the sun, feels delicately for winghold on the sheer fall of sky. He is a tiercel, lean and long and supple-winged, the first of the year. He is the colour of yellow ochre sand and reddish-brown gravel. His big, brown, spaniel eyes shine wet in the sunlight, like circles of raw liver, embedded in the darker matt brown of the moustachial mask. He sweeps away to the west, following the gleaming curve of water. Laboriously I follow his trail of rising plover.

Swallows and martins call sharply, fly low; jays and magpies lurk and mutter in hedges; blackbirds splutter and scold. Where the valley widens, the flat fields are vibrant with tractors. Gulls and lapwings are following the plough. The sun shines from a clear sky flecked with high cirrus. The wind is moving round to the north. By the sudden calling of red-legged partridges and the clattering rise of woodpigeons, I know that the hawk is soaring and drifting southward along the woodland ridge. He is too high to be seen. I stay near the river, hoping he will come back into the wind. Crows in the elms are cursing and bobbing. Jackdaws cackle up from the hill, scatter, spiral away, till they are far out and small and silent in blue depths of sky. The hawk comes down to the river, a mile to the east; disappears into trees he left two hours before.

Young peregrines are fascinated by the endless pouring up and drifting down of the white plume of gulls at the brown wake of the plough. While the autumn ploughing lasts, they will follow the white-bannered tractors from field to field across the valley. They seldom attack. They just like to watch.

That is what the tiercel was doing when I found him again in the alder. He did not move from his perch till one o'clock, when the tractor driver went home to his lunch and gulls settled to sleep in the furrows. Jays were screeching in oaks near the river. They were looking for acorns to bury in the wood. The peregrine heard them, watched their wings flashing white between the leaves. He flew steeply up into the wind, and began to soar. Turning, drifting, swaying, he circled up towards the burning clouds and the cool swathes of sky. I lowered the binoculars to rest my aching arms. As though released, the hawk swept higher and was gone. I scanned the long white spines of cirrus for his thin dark crescent shape, but could not find it. Faint as a whisper, his harsh exultant cry came drifting down.

The jays were silent. One flew heavily up, carrying an acorn in its wide-open bill. Leaving the cover of the trees, it rose high above the meadows, making for the hillside wood four hundred yards away. I could see the big acorn bulging its mandibles apart, like a lemon stuffed in the mouth of a boar's head. There was a sibilant purring sound, like the distant drumming of a snipe. Something blurred and hissed behind the jay, which seemed suddenly to trip and stumble on the air. The acorn spurted out of its bill, like the cork out of a bottle. The jay fell all lopsidedly and threshing, as though it were having a fit. The ground killed it. The peregrine swooped, and carried the dead bird to an oak. There he plucked and ate it, gulping the flesh hastily down, till only the wings, breast-bone, and tail were left.

Gluttonous, hoarding jay; he should have hedge-hopped and lurched from tree to tree in his usual furtive manner. He should never have bared the white flashes of his wings and rump to the watching sky. He was too vivid a mark, as he dazzled slowly across the green water-meadows.

The hawk flew to a dead tree, and slept. At dusk he flew east towards his roosting place.

Wherever he goes, this winter, I will follow him. I will share the fear, and the exaltation, and the boredom, of the hunting life. I will follow him till my predatory human shape no longer darkens in terror the shaken kaleidoscope of colour that stains the deep fovea of his brilliant eye. My pagan head shall sink into the winter land, and there be purified.

October 3rd. Inland stagnant under fog. On the coast: hot sun and cooling breeze, the North Sea flat and shining. Fields of skylarks, singing, chasing, flashing in the sun. Saltings ringing with the redshanks' cry. Shooting, at high tide. Shimmering columns of waders rising from the mud-flats, shaking out across the saltings. White beaches under haze. Waders flashing on the sea like spray, firing the dusty inland fields.

Most of the smaller waders settled on the shell beach: grey plover, knot, turnstone, ringer plover, sanderling. All faced different ways, sleeping, preening, watching, sharp shadowed on the dazzling gritty whiteness of the beach. Dunlin perched on the tips of marsh plants, just above the surface of the tide.

They faced the breeze; stolid, patient, swaying uneasily. There was room for them on the beach, but they would not fly.

Five hundred oystercatchers came down from the south; pied brilliance, whistling through pink bills like sticks of rock. Black legs of sanderling ran on the white beach. A curlew sandpiper stood apart; delicate, foal-like, sea rippling behind it, soft eyes closing in the roan of its face. The tide ebbed. Waders swam in the heat-haze, like watery reflections moored to still, black shadows.

Far out at sea, gulls called. One by one, the larks stopped singing. Waders sank into their shadows, and crouched small. A falcon peregrine, sable on a white shield of sky, circled over from the sea. She slowed, and drifted aimlessly, as though the air above the land was thick and heavy. She dropped. The beaches flared and roared with salvoes of white wings. The sky shredded up, was torn by whirling birds. The falcon rose and fell, like a black billhook in splinters of white wood. She slashed and ripped the air, but could not strike. Tiring, she flew inland. Waders floated down. Cawing rooks flew out to feed on plains of mud.

October 5th. A kestrel hovered beside the brook that separates the flat river plain from the wooded hill. He sank slowly down into stubble, lowering like a threaded spider from the web his wings had spun.

East of the brook, a green orchard rises to the skyline. A peregrine circled high above it, and began to hover. He advanced into the wind, hovering every fifty yards, sometimes staying motionless for a minute or more. The strong west wind was rising to a gale, bending branches, threshing leaves. The sun had gone, and clouds were deepening. The western horizon pricked out black and thorny. Rain was coming. Colour ebbed to brilliant chiaroscuro. Between the narrow edges of his long, level wings, the hawk's down-bent head looked round and bulky as an owl's. A moorhen called, and tinkling goldfinches hid silently in thistles. Magpies hopped into the longer grass, with deep-flexing frog-like bounds. When the orchard ended, the hawk veered away to the north He would not cross the brook while I was there.

He rose upon the wind, and climbed in a narrow spiral, wafting a thousand feet higher with lyrical ease. He skimmed and floated lightly, small and slowly spinning, like a drifting sycamore seed. From far above and beyond the church on the hill, he came down to the orchard again, hovering and advancing into the wind, just as before. His wide-spread tail depressed, his hook-shaped head bent down, his wings curved forward to hug the gale. He crouched upon air, small and huddled, a thousand feet above the orchard trees. Then he uncurled, slowly stretching out his wings and turning on his side. He folded over and down into a steep spiral, suddenly straightening to a vertical dive. He bucked and jerked in air, and dropped between the trees, with long legs swinging down to strike. Dark against the sky, his legs and feet showed thick and sinewy. But it was a clumsy strike, which must have missed, for he rose with nothing in his grasp.

Ten minutes later, a large covey of red-legged partridges left the long grass under the hedge, where they had been hiding, and went back to a patch of bare earth to continue their dust-bathing, which the hawk had disturbed. Partridges can be killed when bathing in this way. The fluttering of their wings draws the eye towards them.

The kestrel hovered over stubble again, and the peregrine swooped at it. Merely a slight, disdainful gesture; yet the kestrel dropped low and flew to the furthest corner of the field, his wings almost touching the stubble.

At three o'clock the drenching rain began. A green sand-piper dwindled up from the brook. Its plaintive, plangent call came chiming back, long after it had woven away into the shining reed-bed of the rain-cloud. Golden plover called in deepening mist. The day seemed over. But as I left the rain-smoked field, the peregrine flew heavily up from the blended mud and straw of the wet soil near the gate. Six partridges followed, and settled in the hedge. As the hawk got smaller, his colour seemed to change from the muddy grey-brown of a curlew to the red-brown and grey-black of a kestrel. He flew heavily, as though waterlogged. I think he had been sitting in the stubble for a long time, waiting for the partridges to rise. He called, and faded over the dim eastern skyline, calling and fading. In the grey mist he looked so like a distant curlew that I half expected to hear the far bugling of a curlew's desolate cry echoing through the harsh staccato chatter of a hawk.

October 7th. The tiercel freed himself from starlings with a rippling slash of wings, and melted up into the mauve haze of the northern sky. Five minutes later he re-appeared, aimed at the river, glided swiftly down into the wind. A falcon flew beside him. Together they glided forward, coming down towards me, beating their wings lightly, then gliding. In ten seconds they had descended from a thousand feet to two hundred, and were passing overhead. The tiercel was more slender and rakish in outline than the falcon. Seen from beneath, their wings were wide across the secondaries, where they joined the body. The falcon's width of wing was equal to more than half her body length. Their tails were short. The outstretched length of head and neck in front of their wings was only slightly less than the length of body and tail behind the wings, but the breadth was twice as great. This gave them an oddly heavy-headed look. I describe these effects in detail, because they can only be observed when peregrines are gliding directly above. Peregrines are more often seen at flatter angles, or in profile, when the proportions seem quite different. The head then looks blunter, the tail longer, the wings less wide.

Evanescent as flame, peregrines sear across the cold sky and are gone, leaving no sign in the blue haze above. But in the lower air a wake of birds trails back, and rises upward through the white helix of the gulls.

The sun shone warmer as the wind grew cold. Woods floated clear along the ridge. The cedars of the big house lawns began to burn and smoulder into dark green light.

At the side of the lane to the ford, I found a long-tailed field mouse feeding on a slope of grass. He was eating the grass seeds, holding the blades securely between his skinny white front paws. So small, blown over by the breath of passing cars, felted with a soft moss of green-brown fur; yet his back was hard and solid to the touch. His long, delicate ears were like hands unfolding; his huge, night-seeing eyes were opaque and dark. He was unaware of my touch, of my face a foot above him, as he bent the tree-top grasses down to his nibbling teeth. I was like a galaxy to him, too big to be seen. I could have picked him up, but it seemed wrong to separate him now from the surface he would never leave until he died. I gave him an acorn. He carried it up the slope in his mouth, stopped, and turned it round against his teeth, flicked it round with his hands, like a potter spinning. His life is eating to live, to catch up, to keep up; never getting ahead moving always in the narrow way between a death and a death; between stoats and weasels, foxes and owls, by night; between cars and kestrels and herons by day.

For two hours, a heron stood at the side of a field, by the hedge, facing the furrowed stubble. He was hunched, slumped, and drooping, on the long stilts of his legs. He shammed dead. His bill moved only once. He was waiting for mice to come and be killed. None came.

Along the brook a tern was hunting, looking down for the flash of a fish at the edge of his dark reflection. He hovered, and plunged into the shallows; rose with a roach in his bill. Twice he dropped it, and spiralled down to catch it again before it hit the water. Then he swallowed it in four large gulps. He glided down, and drank from the brook, running his lower mandible through the surface of the water, slicing out a long, clear ripple.

As the tern rose, the peregrine stooped, whining down from the empty sky. He missed, swept up, and flew off. In the crown of a hollow tree I found three of his kills; a starling, a skylark, and a black-headed gull.

October 8th. Fog lifted. The estuary hardened into shape, cut by the east wind. Horizons smarted in the sun. Islands grew upon the water. At three o'clock, a man walked along the sea-wall, flapping with maps. Five thousand dunlin flew low inland, twenty feet above his head. He did not see them. They poured a waterfall of shadow on to his indifferent face. They rained away inland, like a horde of beetles gleamed with golden chitin.

The tide was high; all waders flew inland; slowly the saltings drifted down beneath the glassy water. Funnels of waders tilted onto inland fields. I crept towards them along a dry ditch, inching forward like the tide. I crawled across stubble and dry plough. A frieze of curlew stood along the skyline, turning their narrow long-billed heads to watch and listen. A pheasant spurted from the dust. The curlew saw me, and glided behind the ridge, but the small waders did not move. They were a long white line on the brown field, like a line of snow. A shadow curved across in front of me. I looked up, and saw a falcon peregrine circling overhead. She kept above me as I moved nearer to the waders, hoping I would put them up. She may have been uncertain what they were. I stayed still, crouching like the waders, looking up at the dark crossbow shape of the hawk. She came lower, peering down at me. She called once: a wild, skirling, 'airk, airk, airk, airk, airk.' When nothing moved, she soared away inland.

There were at least two thousand waders facing me across the furrows, like toy soldiers formed up for battle. Their whiteness was chiefly the white crowns and faces of grey plover. Many dunlin were asleep; turnstones and knot were drowsy; only the godwits were restless and alert. A greenshank flew over, calling monotonously for a long time, making the small waders very uneasy. They reacted as they would to a hawk. Red-legged partridges walked among them, bumping into dunlin, jostling turnstones. They walked forward, or stopped and fed. When a wader would not move, they tried to walk over it. For a bird, there are only two sorts of bird: their own sort, and those that are dangerous. No others exist. The rest are just harmless objects, like stones, or trees, or men when they are dead.

October 9th. Fog hid the day in steamy heat. It smelt acrid and metallic, fumbling my face with cold decaying fingers. It lay by the road like a jurassic saurian, fetid and inert in a swamp.

As the sun rose, the fog shredded and whirled and died away under bushes and hedges. By eleven o'clock the sun was shining from the centre of a great blue circle. Fog burned outwards from its edge, like a dwindling white corona. Colour flamed up from the kindled land. Skylarks sang. Swallows and martins flew downstream.

North of the river, ploughs were turning the heavy earth to smoke and glisten in the sun. From a distant coil of birds the peregrine shook free, and rose into the morning sky. He came south, beating and gliding up in the first frail thermal of the day, circling in figures of eight, curving alternately to left and right. Mobbed by starlings, and rising among them, he passed above me, very high and small, turning his head from side to side and looking down. His large eyes flashed white between the dark bars of his face. The sun bronzed the splendid stubble-coloured brown and yellow hawk, and gleamed his clenched feet to sudden gold. His spread tail stood stiffly out; twelve brown feathers with ten blue strips of sky between.

His circling stopped, and he darted quickly forward, plunging through sunlight. Starlings poured back like jets of smoke, to diffuse and drift to earth. The hawk flew on, into the shining mist-cloud of the south.

He went too fast for me to follow him. I stayed in the valley with partridges and jays, watching skylarks and lapwings come in from the coast. Red-legged partridges had a good breeding season; their coveys are larger and more numerous than ever. Jays abound. I saw eight of them flying across the river, each with an acorn in its bill. They have learnt nothing from the death they saw a week ago; nor has the peregrine learnt how to exploit their folly. Perhaps he found jay meat stringy or insipid. He returned in the late afternoon, but he did not stay. He glided between lombardy poplars, like a full-fed pike between reeds.

October 12th. Dry leaves wither and shine, green of the oak is fading, elms are barred with luminous gold.

There was fog, but the south wind blew it away. The sunburnt sky grew hot. Damp air moved over dusty earth. The north was a haze of blue, the south bleached white. Larks sang up into the warmth, or flashed along furrows. Gulls and lapwings drifted from plough to plough.

Autumn peregrines come inland from the estuaries to bathe in the stony shallows of brook or river. Between eleven o'clock and one they rest in dead trees to dry their feathers, preen, and sleep. Perching stiff and erect, they look like gnarled and twisted oak. To find them, one must learn the shapes of all the valley trees, till anything added becomes, at once, a bird. Hawks hide in dead trees. They grow out of them like branches.

At midday I flushed the tiercel from an elm by the river. Against brown fields, brown leaves, brown mist low to the skyline, he was hard to see. He looked much smaller than the two crows that chased him. But when he rose against the white sky he was bigger, and easier to focus. Quickly he circled higher, slewing away from his course at sudden tangents, baffling the clumsy crows. They always overshot him, and laboured heavily to regain the distance lost. They called, rolling out the 'r's' of their guttural high-pitched 'prruk, prruk', their hawk-mobbing cry. When mobbed, the peregrine beats its wings deeply and rhythmically. They bounce from the air, with silent slaps, like a lapwing's. This deliberate pulse of evasion is beautiful to watch; one breathes in time to it; the effect is hypnotic.

The tiercel turned and twisted in the sun. The undersides of his wings flashed in sword-glints of silver. His dark eyes shone, and the bare skin around them glittered like salt. At five hundred feet the crows gave up, planing back to the trees on outspread wings. The hawk rose higher, and flew fast to the north, gliding smoothly up and round into long soaring circles, till he was hidden in blue haze. Plover volleyed from the fields and fretted the horizon with the dark susurrus of their wings.

Throughout the glaring afternoon, I sat at the southern end of the big field by the river. The sun was hot on my back, and the dry sand-and-clay coloured field shimmered in desert haze. Partridge coveys stood out upon the shining surface like rings of small black stones. When the peregrine circled above them, the partridge rings shrank inward. Lapwings rose and fled. They had been hidden in the furrows, as the hawk was hidden in the shiny corrugations of the sky.

Crows flew up again to chase the hawk away, and the three birds drifted east. Dry feathered and more buoyant now, the tiercel did not beat his wings, but simply soared in the abundant warmth of air. He dodged easily the sudden rushes of the crows, and swooped at them with waggling snipey wings. One crow planed back to earth, but the other plodded on, beating heavily round, a hundred feet below the hawk. When both were very small and high above the wooded hill, the hawk slowed down to let the crow catch up. They dashed at each other, tangling and flinging away, swooping up to regain the height they lost. Rising and fighting, they circled out of sight. Long afterwards the crow came floating back, but the hawk had gone. Half-way to the estuary I found him again, circling among thousands of starlings. They ebbed and flowed about him, bending and flexing sinuously across the sky, like the black funnel of a whirlwind. They carried the tormented hawk towards the coast, till all were suddenly scorched from sight in the horizon's gold corona.

The tide was rising in the estuary; sleeping waders crowded the saltings; plover were restless. I expected the hawk to drop from the sky, but he came low from inland. He was a skimming black crescent, cutting across the saltings, sending up a cloud of dunlin dense as a swarm of bees. He drove up between them, black shark in shoals of silver fish, threshing and plunging. With a sudden stab down he was clear of the swirl and was chasing a solitary dunlin up into the sky. The dunlin seemed to come slowly back to the hawk. It passed into his dark outline, and did not re-appear. There was no brutality, no violence. The hawk's foot reached out, and gripped, and squeezed, and quenched the dunlin's heart as effortlessly as a man's finger extinguishing an insect. Languidly, easily, the hawk glided down to an elm on the island to plume and eat his prey.

October 14th. One of those rare autumn days, calm under high cloud, mild, with patches of distant sunlight circling round and rafters of blue sky crumbling into mist. Elms and oaks still green, but some now scorched with gold. A few leaves falling. Choking smoke from stubble burning.

High tide was at three o'clock, lifting along the southern shore of the estuary. Snipe shuddering from the dykes. White glinting water welling in, mouthing the stones of the sea-wall. Moored boats pecking at the water. Dark red glasswort shining like drowned blood.

Curlew coming over from the island in long flat shields of birds, changing shape like waves upon the shore, long 'V's' widening and narrowing their arms. Redshanks shrill and vehement; never still, never silent. The faint, insistent sadness of grey plover calling. Turnstone and dunlin rising. Twenty greenshank calling, flying high; grey and white as gulls, as sky. Bar-tailed godwits flying with curlew, with knot, with plover; seldom alone, seldom settling; snuffling eccentrics; long-nosed, loud-calling sea-rejoicers; their call a snorting, sneezing, mewing, spitting bark. Their thin upcurved bills turn, their heads turn, their shoulders and whole bodies turn, their wings waggle. They flourish their rococo flight above the surging water.

Screaming gulls corkscrewing high under cloud. Islands blazing with birds. A peregrine rising and falling. Godwits ricocheting across water, tumbling, towering. A peregrine following, swooping, clutching. Godwit and peregrine darting, dodging; stitching land and water with flickering shuttle. Godwit climbing, dwindling, tiny, gone: peregrine diving, perching, panting, beaten.

Tide going out, wigeon cropping zostera, herons lanky

in shallows. Sheep on the sea-wall grazing. Revolve the long estuary through turning eyes. Let the water smooth out its healing line, like touch of dock on nettled finger. Leave the wader-teeming skies, soft over still water, arched light.

October 15th. Fog cleared quickly after one o'clock, and sun shone. The peregrine arrived from the east an hour later. It was seen by sparrows, lapwings, starlings, and woodpigeons, but not by me. I watched and waited in a field near the ford, trying to be as still and patient as the heron that was standing in stubble and waiting for mice to run within reach of his down-chopping bill. Bullfinches called by the brook; swallows flickered round my head. A covey of magpies muttered in hawthorns and then dispersed, dragging up their baggy broomstick tails, catapulting themselves forward from each flurry of wingbeats, sagging on to air at the angle of a well-thrown discus. Thousands of starlings came into the valley to gather by the river before flying to roost.

At half-past four, blackbirds began to scold in the hedges, and red-legged partridges called. I scanned the sky, and found two peregrines—tiercel and falcon—flying high above the ford, chased by crows. The crows soon gave up, but the peregrines flew round for another twenty minutes, in wide random circles. They made many abrupt-angled turns, so that they were never more than a quarter of a mile from the ford. They flew with deep, measured wingbeats—the tiercel's quicker than the falcon's—but they did not move fast. The tiercel flew higher, and constantly swooped down at the falcon, shuddering his wings violently. She avoided these rushes by veering slightly aside. Sometimes both birds slowed till they were almost hovering; then they gradually increased their speed again.

The detail of their plumage was difficult to see, but their

moustachial bars seemed as prominent at a distance as they did when close. The falcon's breast was golden tinted, barred laterally with blackish brown. Her upper parts were a blend of blue-black and brown, so she was probably a second winter bird moulting into adult plumage.

This was the peregrines' true hunting time; an hour and a half to sunset, with the western light declining and the early dusk just rising above the eastern skyline. I thought at first that the peregrines were ringing up to gain height, but they went on circling for so long that obviously some sort of sexual pursuit and display was involved. The birds around me believed they were in danger. Blackbirds and partridges were never silent; woodpigeons, lapwings, and jackdaws scattered from the fields and left the area completely; mallard flew up from the brook.

After twenty minutes the hawks began to fly faster. They rose higher, and the tiercel stopped swooping at the falcon. They circled once, at great speed, and then flew east without turning back. They flickered out of sight towards the estuary, vanishing into the grey dusk a thousand feet above the hill. They were hunting.

October 16th. Waders slept in the spray that leapt from the waves along the shingle ridges. They lined the hot furrows of the inland fields, where dust was blowing. Dunlin, ringed plover, knot and turnstone, faced the wind and sun, clustered together like white pebbles on brown earth.

A roaring southerly gale drove waves to lash the high sea-wall, flinging their spray up through the air above. On the lee side of the wall the long, dry grass was burning. Gasps of yellow flame and northward streaming smoke jetted away in the wind. There was a fierce anguish of heat, like a beast in pain. The short grass on top of the wall glowed orange and black; it hissed when the salt spray thudded down. Under a torrid sky, and in the strength of the sun, water and fire were rejoicing together.

When the waders suddenly flew, I looked beyond them and saw a peregrine lashing down from the northern sky. By the high hunched shoulders, and the big head bent between, and the long, flickering shudder-up and shake-out of the wings, I knew that this was the tiercel. He flew straight towards me, and his eyes seemed to stare into mine. Then they widened in recognition of my hostile human shape. The long wings wrenched and splayed as the hawk swerved violently aside.

I saw his colours clearly in the brilliant light: back and secondaries rich burnt sienna; primaries black; underparts ochreous yellow, streaked with arrowheads of tawny brown. Down the pale cheeks the long dark triangles of the moustachial lobes depended from the polished sun-reflecting eyes.

Through the smoke, through the spray, he glided over the wall in a smooth outpouring, like water gliding over stone. The waders shimmered to earth, and slept. The hawk's plumage stained through shadows of smoke, gleamed like mail in glittering spray. He flew out in the grip of the gale, flicking low across the rising tide. He slashed at a floating gull, and would have plucked it from the water if it had not flown up at once. He flickered out into the light, a small dark blemish diminishing along the great sword of sun-dazzle that lay across the estuary from the south.

By dusk the wind had passed to the north. The sky was clouded, the water low and calm, the fires dying. Out of the misty darkening north, a hundred mallard climbed into the brighter sky, towering above the sunset, far beyond the peregrine that watched them from the shore and the gunners waiting low in the marsh.

October 18th. The valley a damp cocoon of mist; rain drifting through; jackdaws elaborating their oddities of voice and flight, their rackety pursuits, their febrile random feeding; golden plover calling in the rain.

When a crescendo of crackling jackdaws swept into the elms and was silent, I knew that the peregrine was flying. I followed it down to the river. Thousands of starlings sat on pylons and cables, bills opening wide as each bird had his bubbly, squeaky say. Crows watched for the hawk, and blackbirds scolded. After five minutes' alertness the crows relaxed, and released their frustration by swooping at starlings. Blackbirds stopped scolding.

The fine rain was heavy and cold, and I stood by a hawthorn for shelter. At one o'clock, six fieldfares flew into the bush, ate some berries, and flew on again. Their feathers were dark and shining with damp. It was quiet by the river. There was only the faint whisper of the distant weir and the soft gentle breathing of the wind and rain. A monotonous 'keerk, keerk, keerk' sound began, somewhere to the west. It went on for a long time before I recognised it. At first I thought it was the squeak and puff of a mechanical water-pump, but when the sound came nearer I realised that it was a peregrine screeching. This saw-like rasping continued for twenty minutes, gradually becoming feebler and spasmodic. Then it stopped. The peregrine chased a crow through the misty fields and into the branches of a dead oak. As they swooped up to perch, twenty woodpigeons hurtled out of the tree as though they had been fired from it. The crow hopped and sidled along a branch till it was within pecking distance of the peregrine, who turned to face it, lowering his head and wings into a threatening posture. The crow retreated, and the hawk began to call again. His slow, harsh, beaky, serrated cry came clearly across to me through a quarter of a mile of saturated misty air. There is a fine challenging ring to a peregrine's call when there are cliffs or mountains or wide river valleys to give it echo and timbre. A second crow flew up, and the hawk stopped calling. When both crows rushed at him, he flew at once to an overhead wire, where they left him alone.

He looked down at the stubble field in front of him, sleepy but watchful. Gradually he became more alert and intent, restlessly clenching and shifting his feet on the wire. His feathers were ruffled and rain-sodden, draggling down his chest like plaited tawny and brown ropes. He drifted lightly to the field, rose with a mouse, and flew to a distant tree to eat it. He came back to the same place an hour later, and again he sat watching the field; solid, hunched, and bulky with rain. His large head inclined downward, and his eyes probed and unravelled and sorted the intricate mazes of stubbled furrows and rank-spreading weeds. Suddenly he leapt forward into the spreading net of his wings, and flew quickly down to the field. Something was running towards the safety of the ditch at the side. The hawk dropped lightly upon it. Four wings fluttered together, then two were suddenly still. The hawk flew heavily to the centre of the field, dangling a dead moorhen from his foot. It had wandered too far from cover, as moorhens so often do in their search for food, and it had forgotten the enemy that does not move. The bird out of place is always the first to die. Terror seeks out the odd, and the sick, and the lost.

The hawk turned his back to the rain, half spread his wings, and began to feed. For two or three minutes his head stayed down, moving slightly from side to side, as he plucked feathers from the breast of his prey. Then both head and neck moved steadily, regularly, up and down, as he skewered flesh with his notched and pointed bill and dragged lumps of it away from the bone by jerking his head sharply upward. Each time his head came up he looked quickly to left and right before descending again to his food. After ten minutes, this up and down motion became slower, and the pauses between each gulp grew longer. But desultory feeding went on for fifteen minutes more.

When the hawk was still, and his hunger apparently satisfied, I went carefully across the soaking wet grass towards him. He flew at once, carrying the remains of his prey, and was soon hidden in the blinding rain. He begins to know me, but he will not share his kill.

October 20th. The peregrine hovered above the river meadows, large and shining in dark coils of starlings, facing the strong south wind and the freshness of the morning sun. He circled higher, then stooped languidly down, revolving as he fell, his golden feet flashing through sunlight. He tumbled headlong, corkscrewing like a lapwing, scattering starlings. Five minutes later he lifted into air again, circling, gliding, diving up to brightness, like a fish cleaving up through warm blue water, far from the falling nets of the starlings.

A thousand feet high, he poised and drifted, looking down at the small green fields beneath him. His body shone tawny and golden with sunlight, speckled with brown like the scales of a trout. The undersides of his wings were silvery; the secondaries were shaded with a horseshoe pattern of blackish bars, curving inwards from the carpal joint to the axillaries. He rocked and drifted like a boat at anchor, then sailed slowly out onto the northern sky. He lengthened his circles into long ellipses, and swept up to smallness. A flock of lapwings rose below him, veering, swaying, breaking apart. He stooped between them, revolving down in tigerish spirals. Golden light leapt from his twisting talons. It was a splendid stoop, but showy, and I do not think he killed.

The river glinted blue, in green and tawny fields, as I followed the hawk along the side of the hill. At one o'clock he flew fast from the north, where gulls were following the

plough. He landed on a post, mettlesome and wild in movement, with the strong wind ruffling the long fleece of feathers
on his chest, yellow-rippling like ripe wheat. He rested for a
moment, and then dashed forward, sweeping low across a
field of kale, driving out woodpigeons. He rose slightly and
struck at one of them, reaching for it with his foot, like a
goshawk. But it was the merest feint, an idle blow that missed
by yards. He flew on without pausing, keeping low, his back
shining in the sun to a rich mahogany roan, the colour of clay
stained with a deep rust of iron oxide.

Leaving the field, he swung up in the wind and glided over
the river, outlined against sunlight. His wings hung loosely
in the glide, with shoulders drooping; they seemed to project
from the middle of his body, more like the silhouette of a
golden plover than a peregrine. Normally the shoulders are so
hunched, and point so far forward, that the length of body and
neck in front of the wings is never apparent.

Beyond the river, he flew to the east, and I did not see him
again. Hundreds of rooks and gulls puffed out of the skyline,
circled and drifted, thinned and subsided, put up by the hawk
on his way to the coast.

Down by the brook I saw my first snipe of the autumn, and
came close to a partridge. The chestnut horseshoe marking on
its breast seemed to stand out in relief, sharp-edged by the rays
of the sun. At half-past two, the falcon peregrine came over
the trees, with a crow in pursuit. She was much the same size
as the crow; her chest was wider and more barrel-shaped than
the tiercel's, her wings wider and less pointed. She circled fast,
eluded the crow, and began to soar. She soared very high
to the east, moving up through the golden-brown, leaf-
clouded sky of the hill and out into the hovering cloud of
light that towered on the distant water.

October 23rd. Many winter migrants have come into the valley since the twentieth. Today there were fifty blackbirds in hawthorns by the river, where before there were only seven.

The morning was misty and still. A starling mimicked the peregrine perfectly, endlessly repeating its call in the fields to the north of the river. Other birds were made uneasy by it; they were as much deceived as I had been. I could not believe it was not a hawk, until I saw the starling actually opening its bill and producing the sound. By listening to the autumn starlings one can tell from their mimicry when golden plover, fieldfares, kestrels, and peregrines arrive in the valley. Rarer passage birds, like whimbrel and greenshank, will also be faithfully recorded.

At two o'clock, twelve lapwings flew overhead, travelling steadily north-westward. Far above them a peregrine flickered. It was a small, light-coloured tiercel, and it may have been migrating with the lapwings.

When the sun emerged from the mist, the tiercel I had seen throughout the month soared above the water-meadows, surrounded by the inevitable swarm of starlings. At three hundred feet he twitched himself away from the circle, flew quickly over the river, and launched forward and down in a long, fast glide. Hundreds of lapwings and gulls rose steeply from the field, and the hawk was hidden among them. He was probably hoping to seize a bird from below, just after it had risen, but I do not think he succeeded. Half an hour later, many black-headed gulls were still circling a thousand feet above the fields. They drifted fast and gracefully round, on still wings, calling as they glided. Each bird circled a few yards from its neighbour, but always in the opposite direction.

In the clear late-afternoon sunlight, woodpigeons, gulls, and lapwings went up at intervals from different parts of the valley as the peregrine circled over the ford and the woods, along the ridge, and back to the river. He followed the gulls from plough to plough till an hour before sunset. Then he left for the coast.

October 24th. The quiet sky brimmed with cloud, the air was cool and calm, the dry lanes brittle with dead leaves. The tiercel peregrine flew above the valley woods, light, menacing, and stiff-winged, driving woodpigeons from the trees. Down by the river, I found his morning kill; a black-headed gull, a glaring whiteness on dark wet ploughland. It lay on its back, red bill open and stiff red tongue protruding. Though feathers had been plucked from it, not much flesh had been eaten.

I went to the estuary, but the tide was low. The water was hidden in the huge scooped-out emptiness of mud and mist, with the calling of distant curlew and the muffled sadness of grey plover. In the drab light a perched kestrel shone like a triangle of luminous copper.

I left early, and reached the lower river again at four o'clock. Small birds were clamouring from the trees in a shrill hysteria of mobbing. The peregrine flew from cover, passing quite close to me, pursued by blackbirds and starlings. I saw the dark moustachial stripes on the pale face, the buttercup sheen of the brown plumage, the barred and spotted under-wings. The crown of his head looked unusually pale and luminous, a golden-yellow lightly flecked with brown. Long-winged, lean, and powerful, the hawk drew swiftly away from the mob, and glided to north of the river.

He returned an hour later, and flew to the top of a tall chimney. Gulls were passing high above the valley, going out towards the estuary to roost. As each long 'V' of gulls went over, the peregrine flew up and attacked them from below, scattering their close formation, slashing furiously at one bird after another. He swept up among them with his wings half folded, as though he were stooping. Then he turned on his back, curved over and under, and tried to clutch a gull in his foot as he passed beneath it. Their violent twisting and turning must have confused him, for he caught nothing, though he tried, at intervals, for more than half an hour. Whether he was wholly serious in his attempts it was impossible to judge.

At dusk, he settled to roost at the top of the two-hundred-foot chimney, ready to attack the gulls again as they went inland at sunrise. This was a well-sited roosting place at the confluence of two rivers, near the beginning of a large estuary, and undisturbed by the shooting of wildfowl. The main coastal hunting places, two reservoirs, and two river valleys, were all within ten miles; less than twenty minutes' flight. (This chimney has since been felled).

October 26th. The field was silent, misty, furtive with movement. A cold wind layered the sky with cloud. Sparrows pattered into dry-leaved hedges, rustling through the leaves like rain. Blackbirds scolded. Jackdaws and crows peered down from trees. I knew the peregrine was in this field, but I could not find him. I traversed it from corner to corner, but flushed only pheasants and larks. He was hidden among the wet stubble and the dark brown earth his colour matched so well.

Suddenly he was flying, starlings around him, rising from the field and mounting over the river. His wings flickered high, with a lithe and vigorous slash, looking supple and many-jointed. Darting and shrugging, he shook starlings from his shoulders, like a dog shaking spray from his body. He climbed steeply into the east wind, then turned abruptly and headed south. Turning in a long-sided hexagon, not circling, he swung and veered and climbed above the bird-calling fields. In the misty greyness he was the colour of mud and straw; dull frozen shades that only sunlight can transform to flowing gold. His erratic mile-long climb, from ground-level to five-hundred feet, lasted less than a minute. It was made without effort; his wings merely rippled and surged back in an easy unbroken rhythm. His course was never wholly straight; he was always leaning to one side or the other, or suddenly rolling and jinking for a second, like a snipe. Over fields where gulls and lapwings were feeding, he glided for the first time; a long slow glide that made many birds sky up in panic. When they were all rising, he stooped among them, spiralling viciously down. But none was hit.

Two jays flew high across the fields when the peregrine had gone. Unable to decide their direction, they clawed along in an odd disjointed way, carrying acorns and looking gormless. Eventually they went back into the wood. Skylarks and corn buntings sang, the sweet and the dry; redwings whistled thinly through the hedges; curlew called; swallows flew downstream. All was quiet till early afternoon, when the sun shone and gulls came circling over, drifting westward under a small fleece of cloud. They were followed by lapwings and golden plover, including a partial albino with broad white wing-bars and a whitish head. All around me there were birds rising and calling, but I could not see the hawk that was frightening them.

Soon afterwards the tiercel flew near me, where I could not help seeing him. Starlings buzzed about his head, like flies worrying a horse. The sun lit the undersides of his wings, and their cream and brown surfaces had a silver sheen. The dark brown oval patches on the axillaries looked like the black 'armpit' markings of a grey plover. There were dark concavities of shadow under the carpal joint of each wing. Only the primaries moved; quick, sculling strokes rippling silkily back from the still shoulders. Two crows flew up, guttural calls coming from their closed bills and jumping throats. They chased the hawk away to the east, pressing him hard, taking it in turns to swoop at him from either side. When he slashed at one of them, the other immediately rushed in from his blind side. He glided, and tried to soar, but there was not enough time. He just had to fly on till the crows got tired of chasing him.

I went to the estuary and found the hawk again, an hour before sunset, circling a mile off-shore. As the gulls came out to roost on the open water, he flew towards them till he was over the saltings and the sea-wall; then he began to attack. Several gulls evaded the stoop by dropping to the water, but one flew higher. The peregrine stooped at this bird repeatedly, diving down at it in hundred-foot vertical jabs. At first he tried to hit it with his hind toe as he flashed past, but the gull always dodged him by flapping aside at the last second. After five attempts he changed his method, stooped behind the gull, curved quickly under and up, and seized it from below. The gull was obviously much more vulnerable to this form of attack. It did not dodge, but simply flew straight up in the path of the hawk. It was clutched in the breast and carried down to the island, with its limp head looking backwards.

October 28th. Beyond the last farm buildings, the smell of the salt and the mud and the sea-weed mingles with the smell of dead leaves and nutty autumn hedges, and suddenly there is no more inland, and green fields float out to the skyline on a mist of water.

At midday I saw a fox, far out on the saltings, leaping and splashing through the incoming tide. On drier ground he walked; his fur was sleek and dark with wetness, his brush limp and dripping. He shook himself like a dog, sniffed the air, and trotted towards the sea-wall. Suddenly he stopped. Looking through binoculars, I saw the small pupils of his eyes contract and dilate in their white-flecked yellow irises. Eyes savagely alive, light smouldering within, yet glitteringly opaque as jewels. Their unchanging glare was fixed upon me as the fox walked slowly forward. When he stopped again, he was only ten yards away, and I lowered the binoculars. He stood there for more than a minute, trying to understand me with his nose and ears, watching me with his baffled, barbaric eyes. Then the breeze conveyed my fetid human smell, and the beautiful roan-coloured savage became a hunted fox again, ducking and darting away, streaming over the sea-wall and across the long green fields beyond.

Wigeon and teal floated in with the tide; waders crowded the tufts of the saltings. A warning puff of sparrows was followed by the peregrine, gliding slowly out above a thousand crouching waders. The elbow-like carpal joints of his wings were curved and enfolded like the hood of a cobra, and were just as menacing. He flew easily, beating and gliding round the bay, casting his shadow on the still and silent birds. Then he turned inland, and flickered low and fast across the fields.

Four short-eared owls soothed out of the gorse, hushing the air with the tiptoe touch of their soft and elegant wings. Slowly they sank and rose in the wind, drifting against the white estuary and the deep green of the grass. Their big heads turned to watch me, and their fierce eyes glowed and dimmed and glowed again, as though a yellow flame burned beyond the iris, and spat out flakes of fire, and then diminished. One bird called; a sharp barking sound, muffled, like a heron calling in its sleep.

The peregrine circled, and stooped at the drifting owls, but it was like trying to hit blowing feathers with a dart. The owls swayed and turned, rocked about in the draught of the stoops, and rose higher. When they were over the water, the peregrine gave up, and planed down to rest on a post near the wall. I think he could have killed one of them by cutting up at it from below, if he could have separated it from the others, but his stoops went hopelessly wide. At four o'clock he flew slowly inland, darkening briefly along the edges of sunlit fields, deepening out into the shadows of trees.

I left the cold, bird-calling calm of the ebb-tide, and went into the brighter inland dusk, where the air was still heavy and warm between the hedges. Woods smelt pungent and aromatic. In the pure amber of the evening light the dreary green of summer burned up in red and gold. The day came to sunset's windless calm. The wet fields exhaled that indefinable autumnal smell, a sour-sweet rich aroma of cheese and beer, nostalgic, pervasive in the heavy air. I heard a dead leaf loosen and drift down to touch the shining surface of the lane with a light, hard sound. The peregrine drifted softly from a dead tree, like the dim brown ghost of an owl. He was waiting in the dusk; not roosting, but watching for prey. The partridge coveys called, and gathered in the furrows; mallard swished down to the stubble to feed; the hawk did not move. I could see his dark shape huddled at the top of an elm, outlined against the afterglow. Below him was the shine of a stream. Snipe called. The hawk roused and crouched forward. Down from the wood on the hill the first woodcock came slanting and weaving. Three more followed. As they dropped to the mud at the side of the stream the hawk crashed among them. There was a sharp hissing and thrumming of wings as hawk and snipe and woodcock raced upward together. They splayed out above the trees, and a woodcock fell, and splashed into the shallows of the stream. I saw his falling bundled shape and long bill turning aimlessly. The hawk stood in water, plucked his prey, and fed.

October 29th. Ground up by the slow bite of the plough, big clods of black-brown earth curved over into furrows, sliced and shiny-solid, sun glinting on their smooth-cut edges. Gulls and lapwings searched the long brown valleys and the dark crevasses, looking for worms, like eagles seeking snakes.

The peregrine sat on a post by the river, ignoring the birds around him, peering down at a dung-heap. He plunged into reeking straw, scrabbling and fluttering, then rose heavily and flew out of sight to the north, carrying a large brown rat.

At one o'clock the sky above the river darkened from the east, and volleys of arrowed starlings hissed overhead. Behind them, and higher, came a heavy bombardment of wood-pigeons and lapwings. A thousand birds strained forward together as though they did not dare to look back. The dull sky domed white with spiralling gulls. Ten minutes later, the gulls glided back to the plough; starlings and sparrows flew down from the trees. Through the sky, across fields, along hedges, over woodland and river, the peregrine had left his unmistakable spoor of fear.

Birds to the north-east stayed longer in cover, as though they were closer to danger. Following the direction of their gaze, I found the hawk skirmishing with two crows. They chased him; he rose steeply above them; they flew down to a tree; he swooped at them, flicking between the branches; they rose, and chased him again. This game was repeated a dozen times; then the hawk tired of it, and glided away down river. The crows flew towards the woods. Crows must feed very early or very late, for I seldom see them feeding in the valley. They spend their time bathing, mobbing, or chasing other crows.

By three o'clock the hawk had become lithe and nimble in flight. His hunger was growing, and his wings were dancing and bounding on the air as he flew from tree to tree. Starlings rose like smoke from the willows, and hid him completely. He mounted clear of them, spread his wings, and sailed. The wind drifted him away, down the valley. He circled slowly under low grey clouds.

It was almost dark when I found the remains of his kill, the feathers and wings of a common partridge, lying on the river-bank five miles downstream. Blood looked black in the dusk, bare bones white as a grin of teeth. A hawk's kill is like the warm embers of a dying fire.

October 30th. The wind-shred banner of the autumn light spanned the green headland between the two estuaries. The east wind drove drenching grey and silver showers through the frozen cider sky. Birds rose from ploughland as a merlin flew above them, small and brown and swift, lifting dark against the sky, dipping and swerving down along the furrows. All brown or stubbled fields shivered and glittered with larks: all green were pied with plover. Quiet lanes brindled with drifting leaves.

On the coast, the gale was bending the trees back through their lashing branches. The flat land was a booming void where nothing lived. Under the wind, a wren, in sunlight among fallen leaves in a dry ditch seemed suddenly divine, like a small brown priest in a parish of dead leaves and wintry hedges, devoted till death.

I went over the hill to the southern estuary. Rain blew across the fields in roaring clouds of spray. Then the sun shone, and a swallow flitted into light. This valley has its own peculiar loneliness. Steep pastures, lined with elms, slope down to flat fields and marshes. The narrow shining estuary diminishes as the lanes descend. The sudden loneliness and peace one sees, far down between the elms, changes to a different desolation when the river-wall is reached.

Jackdaws charred the green slopes to the north with black. Wigeon whistled through the dry rattling of the bleak marsh reeds, a cheerful explosive sound, which only mist and distance can make faint or sad. A dead curlew lay on top of the wall untouched, breast upward, with a broken neck. The jagged ends of bone had pierced the skin. When I lifted the soft damp body, the long wings fell out like fans. The crows had not yet taken the lovely river-shining of its eyes. I laid it back as it was. The peregrine that had killed it could return to feed when I had gone, and its death would not be wasted. On the marsh, a swan—shot in the breast—had been left to rot. It was greasy, and heavy to lift, and it stank. This handling of the dead left a taint upon the splendour of the day, which ended in a quiet desolation of cloud as the wind fell and the sun passed down.

November 2nd. The whole land shone golden-yellow, bronze, and rusty-red, gleamed water-clear, submerged in brine of autumn light. The peregrine sank up into blue depths, luring the flocked birds higher. Constellations of golden plover glinted far above; gulls and lapwings orbited below; pigeons, duck and starlings hissed in shallow air.

A shower cloud bloomed at the northern edge of the valley and slowly opened out across the sky. The peregrine circled beneath it, clenched in dark fists of starlings. Savagely he lashed himself free, and came superbly to the south, rising on the bright rim of the black cloud, dark in the sun-dazzle floating upon it. He came directly towards me, outlined and fore-shortened, and I could see his long wings angling steeply from his rounded head. The inner wings were inclined upward at an angle of sixty degrees to the body, and they did not move; the narrow outer wings curled higher and dipped lightly into air, waving flamboyantly like sculls that touch and feather through a river's gliding skin. He passed above me, and floated up across the open fields. Slowly he drifted and began to soar, shining in the sun like a bar of river gravel, golden-red. The falcon soared to meet him; together they circled out into the glaring whiteness of the south.

When they had gone, hundreds of fieldfares went back to feed in hawthorns by the river. Some stayed in the yellow lombardy poplars, silently watching, noble in the topmost branches, thin bright eyes and fierce warrior faces. The deep blue of the sky was stained with cloud. Slowly its brilliance descended to the earth. Yellow stubble and dark ploughland shone upward with a greater light.

At half-past one the tiercel returned, flying quickly down towards me as I stood among trees by the brook. He is more willing to face me now, less ready to fly when I approach, puzzled perhaps by my steady pursuit. Seven magpies suddenly dashed up from the grass, squawked in alarm like deep-voiced snipe, swirled together like waders, flung themselves into a tree. The peregrine hovered briefly above the place where they had been. Veering and swaying from side to side, beating his wings with great power and careless freedom, he went overhead in a wash of rushing air. Wings pliant as willow, body firm as oak, he had all the spring and buoyancy of a tern in his leaping, darting flight. Below, he was the colour of river mud, ochreous and tawny; above, he had the sheen of autumn leaves, beech and elm and chestnut. His feathers were finely grained and shaded; they shone like polished wood. Trees hid him from me. When I saw him again, he was a hundred feet higher, climbing fast towards the coast. Two hours to sunset, and the tide rising: it seemed likely that he was heading for the estuary. I followed him there an hour later.

The north wind grew, towering over a cold sky, shedding bleak light, hardening the edges of the hills. Rain drifted across the estuary, and islands stood black on striped and silver water. There were fires and shooting to the north, and a rainbow shone. A horseman rode across the marsh and put up the peregrine, which flew north above the smoke of the fires and the crash of the guns. He carried a dead gull. Long after the brown and yellow hawk had merged into the brown and yellow autumn fields I could see the white wings of the gull fluttering in the wind.

November 4th. The sky peeled white in the north-west gale, leaving the eye no refuge from the sun's cold glare. Distance was blown away, and every tree and church and farm came closer, scoured of its skin of haze. Down the estuary I could see trees nine miles away, bending over in the wind-whipped sea. New horizons stood up bleached and stark, plucked out by the cold talons of the gale.

An iridescence of duck's heads smouldered in foaming blue water: teal brown and green, with a nap like velvet; wigeon copper-red, blazoned with a crest of chrome; mallard deep green in shadow but in the sun luminous, seething up through turquoise, to palest burning blue. A cock bullfinch, alighting on a post against the water, seemed suddenly to flame there, like a winged firework hissing up to glory.

For two hours a falcon peregrine hovered in the gale, leaning into it with heavy flailing wings, moving slowly round the creeks and saltings. She seldom rested, and the wind was too strong for soaring. She followed the sea-wall, flying forward for thirty yards, then hovering. Once, she hovered for a long time, and sank to sixty feet; hovered, and sank to thirty feet; hovered and dropped till only a foot above the long grass on the top of the wall. There she stayed, hovering steadily, for two minutes. She had to fly strongly forward to keep in the same place. Then the grass swayed and crumpled as something ran through it, and the hawk plunged down with outspread wings. There was a scuffle, and something ran along the side of the wall to safety in the ditch at the bottom. The falcon rose, and resumed her patient hovering. She was probably hunting for hares or rabbits. I found the remains of both; the fur had been carefully plucked from them, and the bones neatly cleaned. I also found a mallard drake, drab and ignominious in death.

At sunset the tiercel flew above the marsh, pursuing a wisp of snipe. They drummed away down wind, like stones skidding across ice.

November 6th. Morning was hooded and seeled with deep grey cloud and mist. The mist cleared when the rain began. Many birds fled westward from the river, golden plover high among them. Their melancholy plover voices threaded down through the rain the sorrowing beauty of *ultima thule*.

The peregrine was restless and wild as I followed him across the soaking ploughland clay. He flickered lightly ahead of me in the driving rain, flitting from bush to post, from post to fence, from fence to overhead wire. I followed heavily, with a stone of clay on my boots. But it was worthwhile, for he grew tired of flying, and he did not want to leave the fields. After an hour's pursuit, he allowed me to watch him from fifty yards; two hundred yards had been the limit when we started. Perched on a post, he looked back over his shoulder, but when I moved too much, he jumped up and twisted round to face me, without moving his wings. It was done so quickly that another hawk seemed suddenly to appear there.

He soon became restless again. Partridges called, and he flew across to have a look at them, moving his wings with a stiff downcurving jerkiness, as though he were trying to fly like a partridge. When he glided, he glided like a partridge, with bent wings rigid and trembling. He did not attack, and I do not know whether this mimicry was deliberate, unconscious, or just coincidental. When I saw him again, ten minutes later, he flew with his usual loose-limbed panache.

The rain stopped, the sky cleared, and the hawk began to fly faster. At two o'clock he raced away to the east through snaking lariats of starlings. Effortlessly he climbed above them, red-gold shining above black. They ringed up in pursuit, and he dipped neatly beneath them. Beyond the river he swept down to ground level, and starlings rose steeply up like spray from a breaking wave. They could not overtake him. He was running free, wind flowing from the curves of his wings like water from the back of a diving otter. I put up seven mallard from the river. They circled overhead, and to the west, but they would not fly one yard to the east where the hawk had gone. Running across fields, clambering over gates, cycling along lanes, I followed at my own poor speed. Fortunately he did not get too far ahead, for he paused to chase every flock of birds he saw. They were not serious attacks; he was not yet hunting; it was like a puppy frisking after butterflies. Fieldfares, lapwings, gulls, and golden plover, were scattered, and driven, and goaded into panic. Rooks, jackdaws, sparrows, and skylarks, were threshed up from the furrows and flung about like dead leaves. The whole sky hissed and rained with birds. And with each rush, and plunge, and zigzagging pursuit, his playfulness ebbed away and his hunger grew. He climbed above the hills, looking for sport among the spiky orchards and the moss-green oak woods. Starlings rose into the sky like black searchlight beams, and wavered aimlessly about, seeking the hawk. Woodpigeons began to come back from the east like the survivors of a battle, flying low across the fields. There were thousands of them feeding on acorns in the woods, and the hawk had found them. From every wood and covert, as far as I could see, flock after flock went roaring up into the sky, keeping very close, circling and swirling like dunlin. They rose very high, till there were fifty flocks climbing steeply from the hill and dwindling away down to the eastern horizon. Each flock contained at least a hundred birds. The peregrine was clearing the entire hill of its pigeons, stooping at each wood in turn, sweeping along the rides, flicking between the trees, switchbacking from orchard to orchard, riding along the rim of the sky in a tremendous serration of rebounding dives and ascensions. Suddenly it ended. He mounted like a rocket, curved over in splendid parabola, dived down through cumulus of pigeons. One bird fell back, gashed dead, looking astonished, like a man falling out of a tree. The ground came up and crushed it.

November 9th. A magpie chattered in an elm near the river, watching the sky. Blackbirds scolded; the magpie dived into a bush as the tiercel peregrine flew over. Suddenly the dim day flared. He flashed across clouds like a transient beam of sunlight. Then greyness faded in behind, and he was gone. All morning, birds were huddled together in fear of the hawk, but I could not find him again. If I too were afraid I am sure I should see him more often. Fear releases power. Man might be more tolerable, less fractious and smug, if he had more to fear. I do not mean fear of the intangible, the suffocation of the introvert, but physical fear, cold sweating fear for one's life, fear of the unseen menacing beast, imminent, bristly, tusked and terrible, ravening for one's own hot saline blood.

Halfway to the coast, lapwings went up as a hawk flew above them. They kept in small flocks, and soon there were ten flocks in the air together, scattered across a mile of sky. Those that had been up longest flew higher and wider apart, drifting downwind in tremendous circles half a mile across. The most recently flushed stayed lower, wheeling faster and in narrower circles, closely packed, with only small chinks of light between them. When hawks have gone from sight, you must look up into the sky; their reflection rises in the birds that fear them. There is so much more sky than land.

Under sagging slate-grey clouds the estuary at low tide stretched out into the gloom of the east wind. Long moors of mud shone with deep-cut silver burns. The marshes were intensely green. The feet of grazing cattle sucked and shuddered through craters of dark mud. Several peregrine kills lay on the sides of the sea-wall. I found the remains of a dunlin, dead no more than an hour. The blood was still wet inside it, and it smelt clean and fresh, like mown grass. The wings, and the shining black legs, were untouched. A pile of soft brown and white feathers lay beside them. The head, and most of the body flesh, had been eaten, but the white skin—pimply from careful plucking—had been left. It was still in breeding plumage, which would have made it different from the majority of the flock and so more likely to be attacked by a hawk.

Later, a peregrine flew low across the marsh towards the dunlin he had killed not long before. A black-headed gull rose frantically up in front of him, taken by surprise. (Surely 'taken by surprise' must originally have been a hawking term?) The gull was not quite taken, however, for it strove up vertically, with wildly flapping wings. The hawk glided under its breast and wrenched a few feathers away with his clutching foot before sweeping over and beyond. The gull circled high across the estuary, the hawk alighted on the sea-wall. I walked towards him, but he was reluctant to fly. He waited till I was within twenty yards before he went twisting and zigzagging and rolling away in a most spectacular manner, dodging and jinking across the rising tide like a huge snipe. Shaped against the white water, he glided with wings held stiffly upward from his deep chest, as though he were cast in bronze, like the winged helmet of a Viking warrior.

November 11th. Wisps of sunlight in a bleak of cloud, gulls bone-white in ashes of sky. Sparrows shrilling in tall elm hedges near the river.

I moved slowly and warily forward through the flicking

shadows of twigs, and crept from cover to find the tiercel perched on a post five yards in front of me. He looked round as I stopped, and we both went rigid with the shock of surprise. Light drained away, and the hawk was a dark shape against white sky. His sunken, owl-like head looked dazed and stupid as it turned and bobbed and jerked about. He was dazzled by this sudden confrontation with the devil. The dark moustachial lobes were livid and bristling on the pale Siberian face peering from thick furs. The large bill opened and closed in a silent hiss of alarm, puffing out breath into the cold air. Hesitant, incredulous, outraged, he just squatted on his post and gasped. Then the splintered fragments of his mind sprang together, and he flew very fast and softly away, rolling and twisting from side to side in steepling banks and curves as though avoiding gunshot.

Following him across the river meadows and over the fields by the brook, I found eight recent kills: five lapwings, a moorhen, a partridge, and a woodpigeon. Many fieldfares flew up from the grass. Golden plover and lapwing numbers have increased, and there are more gulls and skylarks now than there were a week ago. Fifteen curlew were feeding in stubble near the brook, among large flocks of starlings and house sparrows.

At one o'clock I flushed the hawk from a post by the road. He flew low along a deep furrow of ploughed field to the west, and I saw a red-legged partridge crouching a hundred yards ahead of him. It was looking the other way, oblivious of danger. The hawk glided forward, reached one foot non-chalantly down, gently kicked the partridge in the back as he floated slowly above it. The partridge scrabbled frantically in the dust, wings flurrying, righted itself, stared about as though completely bewildered. The hawk flew on without looking round, and many partridges began calling. He swooped down and kicked another one over as it ran towards the covey. Then he flew off towards the river. Peregrines spend a lot of time hovering over partridges, or watching them from posts and fences. They are intrigued by their endless walking, by their reluctance to fly. Sometimes this playful interest develops into serious attack.

November 12th. Very still the estuary; misty skylines merged into white water; all peaceful, just the talk of the duck floating in with the tide. Red-breasted mergansers were out in the deep water, diving for fish. They suddenly doubled over and down in a forward roll, very neat and quick. They came up, and swallowed, and looked around, water dripping from their bills; alert, dandified, submarine duck.

A red-throated diver, matted with oil, was stranded in a mud-hole. Only its head was visible. It called incessantly, a painful grunting rising to a long moaning whistle.

I walked along the sea-wall between marsh and water. Short-eared owls breathed out of the grass, turning their overgrown, neglected faces, their yellow eyes' goblin glow. A green woodpecker flew ahead, looping from post to post, clinging like moss, then sinking into heavy flight. The marsh echoed with the hoarse complaint of snipe. I found six peregrine kills: two black-headed gulls, a redshank, and a lapwing, on the wall; an oystercatcher and a grey plover on the shingle beach.

An oval flock of waders came up from the south; fast, compact, white wing-bars flashing in dull light: ten black-tailed godwits. They lanced the air with long, swordfish bills, their long legs stretched out behind. They were calling as they flew—a harsh clamorous gobbling, a heathen laughter, like curlew crossed with mallard. They were greenish-brown, the colour of reeds and saltings. They were dry-looking, crackly, bony birds, with everything pulled out to extremes; beautifully funny. They did not land. They circled, and went back to the south. In summer, their breeding plumage glows fiery orange-red. They feed in deep water, grazing like cattle, and their red reflections seem to scorch and hiss along the surface.

From the big marsh pond came the murmur of the teal flock, like a distant orchestra tuning up. They were skidding and darting through the water, skating up ripples, braking in a flurry of spray. They sprang into the air as a peregrine came flickering from inland. By the time he reached the pond they were half-way across the estuary, their soft calls muffled like a chime of distant hounds. The peregrine disappeared. The teal soon came back, swooping and swirling down to the marsh, rising and falling like round stones skimmed across ice, humming, rebounding, vibrating. Gradually they settled to their feeding and musical calling. I moved nearer to the pond. A pair of teal flew up and came towards me in that silly way they have. The duck landed, but the drake flew past. Suddenly realising he was alone, he turned to go back. As he turned, the peregrine dashed up at him from the marsh and raked him with outstretched talons. The teal was tossed up and over, as though flung up on the horns of a bull. He landed with a splash of blood, his heart torn open. I left the hawk to his kill; the duck flew back to the pond.

November 13th. I flushed two woodcock from hornbeam coppice. They had been sleeping under arches of bramble. They rose vertically into sunlight, their wings making a harsh ripping sound, as though they were tearing themselves free. I could see their long down-pointing bills, shining pink and brown; their heads and chests were striped brown and fawn, like sun and shadow on the woodland floor. Their slack legs dangled, then slowly gathered up. Their dark eyes, large and damp, shone brown and gentle. The tops of the hornbeams rattled, twigs swished and snapped. Then the woodcock were free, darting and weaving away above the trees, glowing in the sun like golden roast. Black mud beneath the brambles, where they had squatted side by side, showed the spidery imprint of their feet.

Under pylons, in a flooded field between two woods, I found the remnants of a rook that the peregrine had eaten. The breast-bone was serrated along the keel, where pieces had been nipped out of it by the hawk's bill. The legs were orange, though they should have been black. When so reduced, a rook's frame and skull seem pathetically small compared with the huge and heavy bill.

By four o'clock, hundreds of clacking fieldfares had gathered in the woods. They moved higher in the trees and became silent, facing the sun. Then they flew north towards their roosting place, rising and calling, straggling out in uneven lines, the sun shining beneath them. And far above them, a peregrine wandered idly round the blue cupola of the cooling sky, and drifted with them to the dead light of the north.

Half an hour before sunset I came to a pine wood. It was already dark under the trees, but there was light in the ride as I walked along it from the west. Outside it was cold, but the wood was still warm. The boles of the pines glowed redly under the blue-black gloom of their branches. The wood had kept its dusk all day, and seemed now to be breathing it out again. I went quietly down the ride, listening to the last rich dungeon notes of a crow. In the middle of the wood, I stopped. A chill spread over my face and neck. Three yards away, on a pine branch close to the ride, there was a tawny owl. I held my breath. The owl did not move. I heard every small sound of the wood as loudly as though I too were an owl. It looked at the light reflected in my eyes. It waited. Its breast was white, thickly arrowed and speckled with tawny red. The redness passed over the sides of its face and head to form a rufous crown. The helmeted face was pale white, ascetic, half-human, bitter and withdrawn. The eyes were dark, intense, baleful. This helmet effect was grotesque, as though some lost and shrunken knight had withered to an owl. As I looked at those grape-blue eyes, fringed with their fiery gold, the bleak face seemed to crumble back into the dusk; only the eyes lived on. The slow recognition of an enemy came visibly to the owl, passing from the eyes, and spreading over the stony face like a shadow. But it had been startled out of its fear, and even now it did not fly at once. Neither of us could bear to look away. Its face was like a mask; macabre, ravaged, sorrowing, like the face of a drowned man. I moved. I could not help it. And the owl suddenly turned its head, shuffled along the branch as though cringing, and flew softly away into the wood.

November 15th. Above South Wood, a small stream flows through a steep-sided valley. The northern slope is open woodland, rusty with winter bracken, silvered with birches, green with mossy oak. The southern slope is pasture, unchanged for many years, rich with worms, lined by small hedges, freckled with thick-branched oak. Two hundred lapwings, and many fieldfares, redwings and blackbirds, were listening for worms as I went down to the stream, which was loud in the quiet morning. There was no ploughing in the river valley, and I expected the peregrine to hunt the lapwings in the higher pasture.

A hard tapping sound began, a long way off. It was like a song thrush banging a snail on a stone, but it came from above. In a hedgerow oak, at the tip of a side branch, a lesser spotted woodpecker was clinging to a small twig, hammering a marble gall with his bill, trying to hack out the grub inside it. To the six-inch-long woodpecker this gall was the size a large medicine ball is to a man. He swung about freely on the twig, sometimes hanging upside down, attacking from many angles. His head went back at least two inches, then thudded forward with pickaxing ferocity. His black shining eyes were needle bright as he looked all round the yellow gall. He could not pierce it. He flew to another oak and tried another gall. All morning I heard him tapping his way across the fields. I tapped a gall with my fingernail, and with a sharp stone, but I could not reproduce the woodpecker's loud cracking sound, which was audible a hundred yards away. He was fairly tame, but if I went too near he stopped, and shuffled farther up the branch, returning when I moved back. When jays called in the wood, he stopped hammering, and listened. Lesser spotted woodpeckers are wary of predators; they fly from cuckoos, and take cover from jays and crows.

Jays were noisy all day in the wood, digging up the acorns they buried a month ago. The first to find one was chased by the others. Several woodcock were feeding at the side of the stream, where the flow of water was checked by fallen branches and dead leaves, and I flushed many more from their resting places in the bracken. During the day, they like to lie up on bracken slopes facing south or west, usually near a cluster of sapling chestnuts or small birches, occasionally under holly or pine. Some birds prefer bramble cover to bracken. Woodcock go up suddenly, after one has been standing near them for a time, as little as five yards away. They may wait for a minute or more, till they can bear the uncertainty no longer. You can flush a greater number by making frequent stops. When trudging straight on through the wood, you put up only those directly in your path. Watching its first steep ascent, you can, for a second, capture the woodcock's colour. Held in a sudden yellowness of light, the blended browns and fawns and chestnuts of its back stand out in relief, like a plating of dead leaves. In the middle of the ridged and stripy back, behind the head, there is a tint of greenish bronze, like verdigris. They may seem to go right away into the distance of the wood, but in fact they pitch steeply down to cover as soon as they are screened by trees. A sudden zigzag and downward flop, over open ground, can be deceptive. They may fly low for a time, rising again when out of sight. Thousands of years of escape practice have evolved these crafty ways. It becomes easy to guess where woodcock are resting, but the actual catapulting ejection from bracken or bramble always startles. One is seldom looking in the right direction.

All wormy mud must have its wader. The fugitive woodcock finds his way along the small windings of the brooks and gulleys, past the forlorn ponds and the muddy undrained rides, to his hermitage of bracken.

The 'pee-wit' calls of plover grew louder as the sun declined. Standing among oaks and birches, I saw between the trees the dark curve of a peregrine scything smoothly up the green slope of the valley. Fieldfares fled towards the trees. Some thudded down into bracken, like falling acorns. The peregrine turned and followed, rose steeply, flicked a fieldfare from its perch, lightly as the wind seizing a leaf. The dead bird dangled from a hawk's-foot gallows. He took it to the brook, plucked and ate it by the water's edge, and left the feathers for the wind to sift.

November 16th. The valley was calm, magnified in mist, domed with a cold adamantine glory. Fifty herring gulls flew north along a thin icicle of blue that wedged the clouds apart. Solemn-winged and sombre, moving away into the narrow pincer of blue, they were a splendid portent of the day to come.

By ten o'clock the blue wedge had widened, and defeated clouds were massing in the eastern sky. Lapwings and golden plover circled down to feed in a newly ploughed field near the river. The first rays of the morning sun reached out to the plover, dim in the dark earth. They shone frail gold, as though their bones were luminous, their feathered skin transparent. The peregrine, which had been hunched and drab in the dead oak, gleamed up in red-gold splendour, like the glowing puffed-out fieldfares in bushes by the river.

When I looked away, the peregrine left his perch, and panic began. The southern sky was terraced with mazes of upward winding birds: seven hundred lapwings, a thousand gulls, two hundred woodpigeons, and five thousand starlings, dwindled up in spiral tiers and widening gyres. Three hundred golden plover circled above them all, visible only when they turned and glinted in the sun. Eventually I found the hawk in the last place I thought of looking—which should have been the first—directly above my head.

He flew southward, rising: four light wing-beats and then a glide, an easy rhythm. Seen from below, his wings seemed merely to kink and straighten, kink and straighten, twitching in and out like a pulse. A crow chased him, and they zig-zagged together. As he rose higher the hawk flew faster; but so light and deft was his wing flicker that he looked to be almost hovering, while the crow moved backwards and down. He fused into the white mist of the sun, and a mass of starlings rose to meet him, as though sucked up by the vortex of a whirlwind. He began to circle at great speed, swinging narrowly round, curving alternately to left and right, sweeping through intricate figures of eight. The starlings were baffled by his sharp twists and turns. They rushed wildly behind him, overshooting the angular bends of his flight. He seemed to swing them around on a line, shaking them out and drawing them in, at will. They all climbed high to the south and were suddenly gone, expunged in mist. This evasion flight—which the hawk seems to enjoy as a form of play, and could so easily escape if he wished—is similar to one of his ways of hunting, and is greatly feared by the birds below. Starlings not actually mobbing sky up violently. They fly to trees or whirl away down wind.

An hour later, there was panic again to the south and west. Plover and gulls spiralled above, blackbirds scolded, cockerels called from farms half a mile apart. The peregrine drifted down to the dead oak to perch, and the calling birds were silent. He rested, preened, and slept for a while, then flew across the open fields north of the river. Tractors were ploughing, and hundreds of gulls were scattered on the black-brown earth, like white chalk. A few sere stubbles still shine between the crinkled darkness of the ploughlands, but the elms are bare, and the poplars tattered yellow. Beagles were silently webbing out on to the wet surface of the fields. Huntsmen and followers were still and waiting. The hare was an acre away, sitting boldly in a furrow, big slant eyes shining in the sun, long ears bending and listening to the wind. The falcon flew up, and hovered above the hare. A distant shot made her flinch and lose height, as though she had been hit. She dropped down, and flew fast and low across the fields. I have never seen a hawk fly lower. Where the headland grass was long, she brushed it with her wings as she passed over. She was hidden by every dip and undulation of the ground. She disappeared along ditches, fanning the long grass outward, flying with her wings bent up, so that the keel of her breast-bone sheared the grass or skimmed an inch above the ground. Suddenly she seemed to fly straight into the furrows. There was no perching place within a quarter of a mile of the spot where she vanished, but I could not find her again, though I diligently quartered every field. Subtle as a harrier, soft-winged as an owl, but flicking along at twice their easy speed, she was as cunning as a fox in her use of cover and camouflage. She clings to the rippling fleece of the earth as the leaping hare cleaves to the wind.

All the gulls left the fields and spiralled silently away to the

south. Cinctures of golden plover glittered round the clear
zenith of the ice-blue sky. The sun was free of the mist at last,
the rising north wind very cold. Beagles had scented the hare
and were streaming over the leaf-stained plough, the hunt
running behind, and the horn sounding. The tiercel circled
low to the north, looking like a tawny kite cut from the earth
beneath him, yellow as stubble, barred with dark brown. He
rose slowly, and drifted down wind. The falcon flew up to
join him, and they circled together, though not in the same
direction. He moved clockwise, she anti-clockwise. Their
random curving paths twined and intersected, but never
matched. As they came nearer to the river, where I was
standing, they quickly rose higher. Both were burnished by
sunlight to a warm red-gold, but the falcon had browner
plumage and was less luminous. They sailed overhead, three
hundred feet up, canting slowly round on still and rigid wings,
the tiercel thirty feet above the falcon. They stared down at
me, with their big heads bent so far under that they appeared
small and sunken between the deep arches of their wings.
With feathers fully spread, and dilated with the sustaining air,
they were wide, thick-set, cobby-looking hawks. The thin,
intricate mesh of pale brown and silver-grey markings over-
laying the buff surfaces of their underwings contrasted with the
vertical mahogany-brown streaks on the deep amber yellow of
their chests. Their clenched feet shone against the white tufts of
their under-tail coverts. The bunched toes were ridged and
knuckled like golden grenades.

They moved to the south of the river, and red-legged
partridges began calling. Each hawk swung up into the wind,
poised briefly, then drifted down and around in a long sweeping circle. Twice the tiercel swooped playfully at the falcon,
almost touching her as he flicked past. He was the shorter in
length by two to three inches, and the lighter in build, with
relatively longer wings and tail. He had grace and slender

strength, she power and solidity. As they dwindled higher, and farther to the south, perspective flattened their circles down to ellipses, and then to straight lines, gliding incisively to and fro across the sky. Their course seemed curiously inevitable, as though they were moving on hidden wires, or following some familiar pathway through the air. It is this beautiful precision, this feeling of pre-ordained movement, that makes the peregrine so exciting to watch.

Now the tiercel drew steadily away from the falcon, rising to the east, while she curved round to the west, and kept lower. Between circles she stayed motionless in the wind. From one of these pitches she turned away as usual, then slanted downwards. Something contained and menacing in her movement made me realise at once that she was going to stoop. She swept down and round in a spiral, wings half bent back, glancing down through the air, smoothly and without haste, at a forty-five degree angle. In this first long curving fall she slowly revolved her body on its axis, and just as the full turn was completed, she tilted over in a perfect arc and poured into the vertical descent. There was a slight check, as though some tenuous barrier of unruly air had been forced through; then she dropped smoothly down. Her wings were now flung up and back and bending inwards, quivering like fins in the gale that rushed along her tapering sides. They were like the flights of an arrow, rippling and pluming above the rigid shaft. She hurled to earth; dashed herself down; disappeared.

A minute later she rose unharmed, but without prey, and flew off to the south. Against blue sky, white cloud, blue sky, dark hills, green fields, brown fields, she had flashed lightly, shone darkly, wheeling and falling. And suddenly the cold, breath-catching air seemed very clear and sweet. The calling of small birds blended with the chiming bark of the beagles and the thudding away of the hunted hare. It streamed through a hedge and flung into the river, splashing in like a spadeful of brown earth. It swam to the far bank, and limped away to safety.

Where the tiercel still circled to the east, the sky was drifted with gulls and plover and curlew. The sharp glinting speck of the hawk faded slowly out above the hills, sweeping majestically towards the sea. The alarmed birds descended, and the great flight was over.

I followed the falcon, and found her again at half past three. Smoked out by dense clouds of starlings, she flew from the ash tree by ford lane pond and flickered low across fields where tractors were working and sugar beet was being cut and carted. Where the ground had been cleared, hundreds of gulls and lapwings were feeding; I lost the hawk among them as they rose. Ten minutes later she flew north-east, passing high towards the river, black against the lemon-yellow sky. She veered to the east, flying higher and faster, as though she had sighted prey.

The beagles are going home along the small hill lanes, the huntsmen tired, the followers gone, the hare safe in its form. The valley sinks into mist, and the yellow orbital ring of the horizon closes over the glaring cornea of the sun. The eastern ridge blooms purple, then fades to inimical black. The earth exhales into the cold dusk. Frost forms in hollows shaded from the afterglow. Owls wake and call. The first stars hover and drift down. Like a roosting hawk, I listen to silence and gaze into the dark.

November 18th. In the morning I walked east along the sea-wall, from the estuary to the sea. The water was pale grey and white under high cloud. It became seamed and veined with blue as the sky cleared and the sun came out. Waders, gulls and rooks fed by the tide-line. Bushes near the wall were full of larks and finches. Three snow buntings ran over the white shingle and sand, like waders, unwilling to fly, brown and white as the sand beneath them. When they ran on to darker ground, they flew at once, calling. Their long white-barred wings flashed up into sunlight, their hard, pure calls chimed faintly down.

All morning, I had the wary, uneasy feeling that comes when a hawk is near. I felt that he was hidden just beyond sight; in time and distance barely outpacing me, always dropping below the horizon as I moved up over the curve of the flat green land. By one o'clock I was heading south, and the sun was dazzling. Suddenly I seemed to be walking away from the hawk instead of towards it. I went down into the fields and across to the estuary again, not thinking, moving only on the rim of thought, content to see and absorb the day. Turning through a hedge-gap, I surprised a wren. It trembled on its perch in an agony of hesitation, not knowing whether to fly or not, its mind in a stutter, splitting up with fear. I went quickly past, and it relaxed, and sang.

At half past two I reached the estuary. It was high tide. White gulls floated on blue unclouded water, duck slept, waders crowded the saltings. I walked slowly west along the sea-wall. It was now the ebb-light of a cold November day, and the western sky was frosted with pale gold. That radiant arch of light, which curves up and over the flat river land from the North Sea beyond it, was crumbling at the zenith and flaking back to grey. This was the last true hunting light, a call as clear to the hungry hawk as the 'gone away' of a huntsman's horn.

A low stream of dunlin left the saltings and swelled upon the water to a glittering silver sail, billowing out towards the island. Above, and far beyond them, a peregrine was flying, a small dark knuckle in the flawless sky. Swiftly it grew to a dart of flickering wings. It rose black and sharp against the sun, and then it was beyond the sun and was browner and less menacing. It dived, and the island birds were flung up like spray. It circled above them, and they fell back like a wave. In steeply rising rings the hawk mounted to a silent crescendo. Gulls flew up. It stopped above them, poised, then dived downward, sweeping down and under and up again in a great 'U'-shaped curve, cleaving the air as a human diver cleaves through air and water. From the reaching talons a gull flopped gracelessly aside. The peregrine rose higher, and shivered out into the greying eastern sky.

In the bright west, in long streams above the estuary calm, a thousand lapwings wheeled and feathered in their changing squadrons, their soft wings rising and falling in rhythm like the oars of a long-boat.

November 21st. A wrought-iron starkness of leafless trees stands sharply up along the valley skyline. The cold north air, like a lens of ice, transforms and clarifies. Wet ploughlands are dark as malt, stubbles are bearded with weeds and sodden with water. Gales have taken the last of the leaves. Autumn is thrown down. Winter stands.

At two o'clock a crackling blackness of jackdaws swept up from stubble and scattered out across the sky with a noise like dominoes being rattled together on a pub table. Woodpigeons and lapwings rose to the south. The peregrine was near, but I could not see it. I went down to the brook and across the fields between the two woods. From stubble and plough I flushed gleanings of skylarks. The sun shone. Trees coloured like tawny gravel on the bed of a clear stream. The oaks of the two woods were maned with spiky gold. A green woodpecker flew from the wet grass and clapped itself to the bole of a tree as though pulled in by a magnet. Above the moss and mustard of its back, the crown of its head smouldered vermilion, like scarlet agaric shining through a dark wood. The high, harsh alarm call came loud and sudden, a breathless squeezed-out sound, meaning 'hawk sighted.' In the bare spars of the limes by the bridge, silent fieldfares were watching the sky.

I looked to the west, and saw the peregrine moving up above the distant farmhouse cedar, luminous in a dark cloud of rooks, drifting in streams of golden plover. A black shower cloud was glooming from the north; the peregrine shone against it in a nimbus of narrow gold. He glided over stubble, and a wave of sparrows dashed itself into a hedge. For a second, the hawk's wings danced in pursuit, flicking lithe and high in a cluster of frenzied beats that freeze in memory to the shape of antlers. Then he flew calmly on towards the river.

I followed, but could not find him. Dusk and sunset came together in the river mist. A shrew scuffled in dead leaves beneath a hedge, and hid among them when a little owl began to call. Water voles, running along the branch of a bush that overhangs the river, were suddenly still when they heard the call. When it stopped, they dived into the water and swam into the cover of the reeds. I walked along beside the hedge. A woodcock startled me by its sudden, noisy, upward leaping. It flew against the sky, and I saw the long downward-pointing bill and the blunt owl-like wings, and heard the thin whistle and throaty croak of its roding call; a strange thing to hear in the cold November dusk. It wavered away to the west, and the peregrine starred above it, a dark incisive shape descending through the pale saffron of the afterglow. They disappeared into the dusk together, and I saw nothing more.

November 24th. A peregrine soared above the valley in the morning sunshine and the warm south breeze. I could not see it, but its motion through the sky was reflected on the ground beneath in the restless rising of the plover, in the white swirl of gulls, in the clattering grey clouds of woodpigeons, in hundreds of bright birds' eyes looking upward.

When all was quiet, tiercel and falcon flew low and side by side across the wide plain of the open fields. Moving up wind, they scattered golden plover from the stubble. They were coloured like plover themselves and were soon hidden in the tawny-brown horizon of the fields.

Rain-clouds thickened and lowered, wind rose, everything became sharp-edged. I disturbed the falcon from an oak near ford lane. She flew quickly away to the north-east, rose beyond the brook, and hovered over the orchard. Between hovers she glided and circled, trying to soar, but she could not do so. Slowly she drifted over the hill to the east. There was no panic among the orchard birds, but many fieldfares and finches flew up and straggled aimlessly about beneath the hawk as though unable to decide whether to mob it or not. Most birds find a hovering peregrine difficult to understand. As soon as it flies fast, they know what they have to do, but when it hovers like a kestrel they are less perturbed. The only birds that immediately recognise it as being dangerous are partridges and pheasants. They are the species most threatened by this manner of hunting, and they either crouch low or run to the nearest cover. Hovering kestrels they ignore.

I went across the fields to the south of the lane, and put up three curlew. There were four there on the 21st; a peregrine may have killed the other one since then. As the curlew flew off, calling, the tiercel appeared, a hundred yards to the west. Lapwings rose quickly from the stubble in front of him, but they had misjudged the strength of the wind and had risen too late. The tiercel swung steeply up, wind filling his cupped wings like sails. He poised for a moment, then flattened his wings sharply to his sides and rushed downwards, piercing through the wind to the last lapwing of the straggling line. The glancing blow was struck so quickly that I did not see it. I only saw the hawk flying down wind, carrying his kill.

An hour of drenching rain extinguished the day. The

valley was a sopping brown sponge, misty and dun. Sixteen mallard flew over, and a wigeon whistled. Rain fell copiously again, and the hollow dusk was filled with the squelching calls of snipe.

November 26th. Rooks and gulls moving over the rainy town at dawn: rooks to the estuary, gulls to inland. Down by the sound of the tide, corn buntings sang in cottage gardens. Rain blew gently as daylight gained. Waders gathered on the shrinking rim of shore, dark heads against white water. Grey plover were feeding, leaning forward like pointers, listening to the mud like thrushes on a lawn. A careful step, a thrust of the head forward and over, a strained intentness; then the bill darting down through the mud, spearing out a worm, fast and springy as a fencer. Knot were resting. They had a slant-eyed mongol look, like sleeping huskies. Fifty flew out across the water as I stumbled through the sticky clay on the top of the sea-wall. Grey birds, sweeping low under the white-stoned clear horizon and the high grey sky, low to the rain-spattered white of water and the scoured shore, black-purple seaweed, weed-green islands, and long seas heaving smooth.

Six cormorants squatted at the tideline, like blackened tree-stumps. Farther east, one rested with its wings outspread, heraldic against the whole North Sea. Long 'V's' of brent geese flew past. The clucking guttural of their conversation was audible a mile away. Their long black lines clawed along the bottom of the sky.

The wings of hawk kills fluttered on the shingle: a wigeon and six black-headed gulls were old and stale, a red-breasted merganser was only three days dead. It is surprising that a peregrine should kill a merganser, a bird most foul and fishy-tasting to the human palate. Only the wings, bones, and bill, had been left. Even the skull had been picked clean. That narrow saw-billed head, with its serrated prehistoric grin, had been too much to swallow. A falcon peregrine watched me from posts far out on the saltings, sitting huddled and morose under darkening rain. She flew seldom, had fed, had nothing to do. Later, she went inland.

Greenshanks stood in the marsh; hoary-looking waders, grey and mossy coloured, tilting forward to feed over their thin grey legs. Where they were not grey, they were white; bleak, leaden birds, phantoms of summer green, suddenly aloof and beautiful in flight. Slow rain fell from mid-grey, light grey sky. A deceptive clarity and brightening at eleven o'clock meant that the rain was really setting in. For an hour, till greyness covered all, the water shone like milk and mother-of-pearl. The sea breathed quietly, like a sleeping dog.

November 28th. Nothing was clear in the tractor-echoing dreariness of this misty day. The thin and faltering north-west wind was cold.

At eleven o'clock a peregrine flew up to one of the line of tall pylons that extends across the valley. He was blurred in mist, but the deft bowing and fanning of his wings was instantly familiar. For twenty minutes he watched the plover feeding in the surrounding fields, then flew south to the next pylon. There he was silhouetted in an owl shape against the white sky, his sunken head rounding out into high curved shoulders and tapering down to the short blunt-ended tail. He flew north again, moving up above the shining mist-coils of the river, the red-gold burnish of his plumage glowing into dimness. His wings rowed back with long powerful strokes, sweeping him easily, majestically forward.

I could not follow him in such poor light, so I went down to the brook, thinking that later he might come there to bathe. Blackbirds and chaffinches were scolding in the hawthorns by North Wood, and a jay was perching in alders and looking down at something. Keeping in the cover of hedges, I went slowly along to the thick mass of hawthorns. I forced my way into them till I could see the fast-moving water of the brook, which the jay had been watching. Through the dark mesh of thorny twigs, I saw a falcon peregrine standing on stones, a few inches from the water, looking intently at her own reflection. She walked slowly forward till her large, wrinkled yellow feet were immersed. She stopped and glared around, then raised her wings at a steep angle above her back and waded carefully out into the water, stepping gingerly on the small gravelly stones as though afraid of slipping. When the water was nearly up to her shoulders, she stopped. She drank a few sips, dipped her head beneath the surface repeatedly, splashed, dowsed and flapped her wings. Blackbirds and chaffinches stopped scolding, and the jay flew off.

She stayed in the water for ten minutes, gradually becoming less active; then she waddled heavily ashore. Her curious parrot-like amble was made even more ungainly by the weight of water in her feathers. She shook herself a great deal, made little jumps into the air with flailing wings, and flew cumbersomely up into a dead alder that overhangs the brook. Blackbirds and chaffinches started scolding again, and the jay came back. The peregrine was huge with water, and did not look at all happy. She was deeper-chested and broader-backed than the tiercel, with a bigger hump of muscle between her shoulders. She was darker in colour and more like the conventional pictures of young peregrines. The jay began to flutter round her in an irritating manner. She flew heavily away to the north, with the jay screeching derisively in pursuit.

I found her in a dead oak to the north-east of the ford. The tree stands on higher ground, and from its topmost branches a hawk can see for several miles across the open river plain to the west. After looking all around, and up at the sky, she began to preen. She did not raise her head again till she had finished. The breast feathers were preened first; then the undersides of the wings, the belly, and the flanks, in that order. When the preening was done, she picked savagely at her feet, sometimes raising one to get a better grip on it, and cleaned and honed her bill upon the bark of the tree. She slept fitfully till one o'clock, then flew quickly away to the east.

November 29th. At midday a peregrine flew from inland, passing quite close to me as I stood on the sea-wall near the saltings. Beyond the wall it rose, hovered, and swept down and up in savage 'U'-shaped stoops. Three times it did this, then flew back the way it had come. I thought it was trying to flush prey from the shore, but when I reached the place where it had stooped, I found nothing there. It may have been practising its aim at some post or stone, but I do not understand why it should have flown to and from that particular spot in such a deliberate way.

I went on to the east. The sun shone, but the wind was cold; a good soaring day for hawks.

Three hours later I returned to the saltings, and found the remains of a great crested grebe at the foot of the sea-wall, near the high-water mark. It had been a heavy bird, weighing perhaps two and a half pounds, and it was probably killed by a stoop from a considerable height. It now weighed less than a pound. The breast-bone and ribs were bare. The vertebræ of the long neck had also been carefully cleaned. The head, wings, and stomach were untouched. The exposed organs steamed slightly in the frosty air, and were still warm. Although so fresh, they had an unpleasant rancid smell. Grebes taste rank and fishy to the human palate.

At sunset, as I went across the marsh, two peregrines flew from the roof of a hut. Languid and heavy-cropped, they did not fly far. They had shared the grebe, and now they were roosting together.

November 30th. Two kills by the river: kingfisher and snipe. The snipe lay half submerged in flooded grass, cryptic even in death. The kingfisher shone in mud at the river's edge, like a brilliant eye. He was tattered with blood, stained with the blood-red colour of his stumpy legs that were stiff and red as sticks of sealing wax, cold in the lapping ripple of the river. He was like a dead star, whose green and turquoise light still glimmers down through the long light-years.

In the afternoon I crossed the field that slopes up from North Wood, and saw feathers blowing in the wind. The body of a woodpigeon lay breast upward on a mass of soft white feathers. The head had been eaten. Flesh had been torn from the neck, breast-bone, ribs, and pelvis, and even from the shoulder-girdles and the carpal joints of the wings. This tiercel eats well. His butchery is beautifully done. The carcass weighed only a few ounces, so nearly a pound of meat had been taken from it. The bones were still dark red, the blood still wet.

I found myself crouching over the kill, like a mantling hawk. My eyes turned quickly about, alert for the walking heads of men. Unconsciously I was imitating the movements of a hawk, as in some primitive ritual; the hunter becoming the thing he hunts. I looked into the wood. In a lair of shadow the peregrine was crouching, watching me, gripping the neck of a dead branch. We live, in these days in the open, the same ecstatic fearful life. We shun men. We hate their suddenly uplifted arms, the insanity of their flailing gestures, their erratic scissoring gait, their aimless stumbling ways, the tombstone whiteness of their faces.

December 1st. The peregrine soared unseen in the blue zenith of the misty sky, and circled east above the rising coils of gulls. After half an hour of idling through the morning sunshine and drifting in the cold south-east wind, he came down to the brook with tremendous swooping force, bursting up a star of fragment birds. A snipe whistled away down wind like a shell, and the first great clattering of woodpigeons settled to the long sighing of departing wings. Blackbirds were still scolding when I reached the bridge, but the sky was empty. All the trees to southward—stark against the low glare of the sun—were heavy with pigeons, thick clustered like black fruit.

When the slowly relaxing tension, and the uneasy peace, had lasted for twenty minutes, the pigeons began to return to the fields. Gulls and plover went back to following the plough. Migrating lapwings flew high to the north-west, serene and untroubled. Woodpigeons flew between the two woods, and between the woods and the ploughed fields. They were never still, and their white wing-bars flashed in sunlight, a temptation and a challenge to the watching peregrine.

I scanned the sky constantly to see if a hawk was soaring, scrutinised every tree and bush, searched the apparently empty sky through every arc. That is how the hawk finds his prey and eludes his enemies, and that is the only way one can hope to find him and share his hunting. Binoculars, and a hawk-like vigilance, reduce the disadvantage of myopic human vision.

At last, yet one more of all the distant pigeon-like birds, that till then had always proved to be pigeons, was suddenly the peregrine. He flew over South Wood, and soared in the warm air rising from open spaces sheltered by encircling trees. Crisp and golden in the sunlight, he swam up through the warm air with muscular undulations of his wings, like the waving flicker of a fish's fins. He drifted on the surface, a tiny silver flake on the blue burnish of the sky. His wings tightened and bent back, and he slid away to the east, a dark blade cutting slowly through blue ice. Moving down through sunlight, he changed colour like an autumn leaf, passing from shining gold to pallid yellow, turning from tawny to brown, suddenly flicking out black against the skyline.

White fire smouldered in the south as the sun glared lower. Two jackdaws flew high above. One dived, went into a spin, looped the loop, and fell towards earth as though it had been shot, a tossing bag of bones and feathers. It was playing at being dead. When a foot from the ground, it spread its wings and dropped lightly down, superbly nonchalant.

Following the restless plover, I crossed the brook and found the falcon peregrine in a hedge to the west. I stalked her, but she moved from tree to tree along the hedge, keeping up against the sun, where she could see me clearly while I was dazzled. When the hedge ended, she flew to a tree by the brook. She seemed sleepy and lethargic and did not move her head much. Her eyes had a brown ceramic glaze. They watched my eyes intently. I turned away for a moment. She flew at once. I looked back quickly, but she had gone. Hawks are reluctant to fly while they are being watched. They wait till the strange bondage of the eyes is broken.

Gulls flew slowly over to the east, their wings transparent in the brilliant light. At three o'clock the falcon circled among them, and began to soar. It was high tide at the estuary. Waders would be swirling up and sinking down above the creeks and saltings like blood pounding in a caged heart. I knew the peregrine would see them, would see the thousands of gulls moving in towards the brimming water, and I thought she would follow them eastward. Without waiting longer, I cycled as fast as I could across to a small hill, six miles away, that overlooks the estuary. Twice I stopped and searched for the falcon and found her circling high above the wooded ridge, drifting east as I had hoped. By the time I reached the hill she had passed over and down.

In the small lens of light that the telescope cored out from three miles of sunlit intervening air, I saw the shining water of the estuary darken and seethe with birds and the sharp hook of the falcon rising and falling in a long crenellation of stoops. Then the dark water lifted to brightness again, and all was still.

December 2nd. The tide was low. Mud shone like wet sand, and shingle strands were bright and glaring in the blue lagoons. Colour smarted in sunlight. A dead tree in dark fields reflected light, like an ivory bone. Bare trees stood in the earth, like the glowing veins of withered leaves.

A peregrine soared above the estuary, and the sky filled with the wings of waders. He dived through sunlight into a falling darkness of curlew, flashed through them into light again, curved under and rose beneath them as they rose, struck one in the breast with gasping force. It dropped beside the sea-wall, all out of shape, as though its body had been suddenly deflated. The peregrine glided down, and lanced the dead curlew's breast with the hook of his bill.

December 3rd. All day the low clouds lay above the marshes and thin rain drifted in from the sea. Mud was deep in the lanes and along the sea-wall; thick ochre mud, like paint; oozing glutinous mud that seemed to sprout on the marsh, like fungus; octopus mud that clutched and clung and squelched and sucked; slippery mud, smooth and treacherous as oil; mud stagnant; mud evil; mud in the clothes, in the hair, in the eyes; mud to the bone. On the east coast in winter, above or below the tide-line, man walks in water or in mud; there is no dry land. Mud is another element. One comes to love it, to be like a wading bird, happy only at the edges of the world where land and water meet, where there is no shade and nowhere for fear to hide.

At the mouth of the estuary, land and water lose themselves together, and the eye sees only water and land floating upon water. The grey and white horizons are moored on rafts. They move out into the dusk and leave the water-land to the ear alone, to the whistling of the wigeon, the crying of curlew, and the calling of gulls.

There was a hawk to the north, circling over the higher ground and flying to roost. But it was too far off to draw me away from the falling tide. Thousands of gulls came out from the land at evening to the cleanness and safety of the sea.

December 5th. The sun fired the bone-white coral of the frosted hedges with a cold and sullen glow. Nothing moved in the silent valley till the rime melted and steamed in the sun, and trees began to drip through the misty cave that boomed and blurred with voices drifting from the stirring farms. The peregrine flew from a haystack by the road, where he had been resting in the sun, and went down to the river.

Half an hour later I found him near the bridge, perched on an overhead wire. He flew low along a ditch, brushing rime from the stiff reeds with his wings. He twisted, and turned, and hovered above a moorhen. It skidded and threshed on the ice between the reeds, and he could not catch it. Fourteen teal and a hundred gulls flew up from a stretch of unfrozen water. There were many tame and hungry snipe in the frosty fields, feeble, and faintly calling.

At one o'clock the peregrine flew east, rising over the sunlit cliffs of fog on strong, determined wings.

December 8th. Golden leaves of sunlight drifted down through morning fog. Fields shone wet under blue sky. From an elm near the river the tiercel peregrine flew up into the misty sunlight, calling: a high, husky, muffled call: 'keerk,

keerk, keerk, keerk, keerk', sharp-edged and barbarous.

He rose over stubble to the north, keeping the sun behind him, beating forward, mounting in buoyant glides. He had the tenseness and taut ply in his wings that means he has sighted prey. Woodpigeons in the stubble stopped feeding, and raised their heads. Two hundred feet above them the hawk slowly circled, then slanted suddenly over and down. He slashed down through the air and swung up, and the pigeons flew wildly beneath him. He twisted over and down, with a sinuous coiling of wings, and cut in among them, piercing their soft grey hurtling mass.

Birds rose from all the fields around. Whole fields seemed to lift into the sky. Somewhere in this seething of wings the hawk was lost inextricably. When the turmoil subsided, there was no hawk within miles. This happens so often: the stealthy soft-winged approach, the sudden attack, then the hidden departure, concealed in a diffusing smoke-screen of birds.

I reached the estuary at high tide. Thousands of glittering dunlin hissed and plunged over blue water. Brent geese and wigeon floated in the brimming bays. Gunners were out. Through the bronze flashes, and the booming of the early dusk, wigeon whistled unquenchably and a solitary red-throated diver raised its melancholy wail.

The peregrine did not come back to the circling, echoing clangour of the banging estuary. He had killed in the morning, and wisely stayed inland.

December 10th. Bleak light, brutal wind, thickening cloud, showers of sleet. Snipe huddled in a flooded meadow north of the river, like little brown monks fishing. They crouched low over their bent green legs, and I could see their Colorado-beetle-coloured heads and their gentle brown eyes. They did not feed, but simply held their long bills out above the muddy water, as though they were savouring the bouquet. Fifty went up when I walked towards them. There is no hesitation, no slow awakening, for snipe; only the sudden convulsive jump from the mud when the alarm rings in their nerves. They made a tremendous nasal noise as they rose: a sneeze of snipe, not a wisp. They kept close together and did not jink, flying high and fast in a group, like starlings. This meant that a hawk was about.

After much searching I found the tiercel on a post in the fields. He looked sleepy and lethargic. He did not become alert till early afternoon, when light began to fade and misty dusk furred the distant trees. He circled over the meadow where snipe were resting. None rose till he stooped. Then they all spluttered and crackled up from the mud, like damp squibs. The last to rise was chased by the hawk. Together they tore up into the sky, plunged down across the fields, rushed in and out of the willows. The hawk followed every twist and turn, keeping up with the snipe, but never overtaking it. He stopped his pursuit quite suddenly, and dashed at the hundreds of fieldfares that were milling above the river in a random incohesive way. He still flew like a snipe, jinking and bouncing about like an uncoiling spring, scattering fieldfares but not attacking them.

He rested on a post for ten minutes, then flew steadily up wind, keeping very low and half-hidden in the darkening misty fields. His head and tail were invisible. He was like a manta ray flicking along the bottom of the sea. Gulls flew southward towards their roost. They came in fast-moving flocks of thirty or forty, and they would not fly directly overhead. They split up as soon as they saw me, scattering to left or right, like woodpigeons. I had never seen them do that before. Repeated attacks by the peregrine, at morning and evening, had made them very wild, and suspicious of danger from below.

I followed the peregrine to the east. Fieldfares clacked and whistled above me on their way to roost by the river. From a small stream I put up a green sandpiper. It towered into the dusk, calling, veering and swaying about like a tipsy snipe. Its call was a wild, whistling 'too-loo-weet,' indescribably triumphant and forlorn. The peregrine stooped as the sandpiper rose, but he missed it by a yard. He may have been following me so that I could flush prey for him. All the stoops he made today were slow and inaccurate. Perhaps he was not really hungry, but was compelled by habit to practise a ritual of hunting and killing.

The sky cleared after sunset. Far above, there was a sound like a distant striking of matches. Many rooks and jackdaws were calling as they flew slowly, peacefully, westward, high in the cold blue dusk, small as the first stars.

December 12th. High clouds slowly filled the sky, the morning whitened out, the sun was hidden. A cold wind rose from the north. The horizon light became clear and vivid.

The remains of a herring gull lay at the roadside, between two farms, half on the grass verge and half in the dust and grit. The peregrine had killed it in the night, or in the morning dusk, before there was any traffic on the road, and had found it too heavy to carry to a safer place. Since then, the passing cars had squashed it flat. The shredded flesh was still wet with blood, and the neck gaped redly where the head had been. To hawks, these gritty country lanes must look like shingle beaches; the polished roads must gleam like seams of granite in a moorland waste. All the monstrous artifacts of man are natural, untainted things to them. All that is still is dead. All that moves, and stops, and does not move again, then very slowly dies. Movement is like colour to a hawk; it flares upon the eye like crimson flame.

I found the gull at ten o'clock, and the peregrine a quarter of an hour later. As I expected, after eating so large a bird he had not gone far away. Looking very wet and dejected, with feathers loose and bedraggled, he was slumped on a tree by the ford lane pond. His tail dangled beneath him like a sodden umbrella. The pond is small and shallow, and contains the usual human detritus; pram wheels, tricycles, broken glass, rotting cabbages, and detergent containers, overlaid by a thin ketchup of sewage. The water is stagnant and greasy, but the hawk may have bathed in it. Normally he prefers clear running water of a certain depth and quality—and he will fly long distances to find it—but sometimes he seems deliberately to choose water containing sewage.

Three tractors were ploughing in the big field to the south. One of them was passing up and down, a few yards from the hawk, without disturbing him at all. Hawks perch near fields where tractors are working, because that is where birds are constantly on the move. There is always something to watch, or something to kill if the hawk should be hungry. They have learnt that the dreaded man-shape is harmless while the tractor is in motion. They do not fear machines, for a machine's behaviour is so much more predictable than man's. When the tractor stops, the hawk is immediately alert. When the driver walks away, the hawk moves to a more distant perch. This happened in the field by the pond half an hour after I arrived there. The hawk flew slowly south-east, lifting and swinging his wings like heavy unwieldy oars, and drifted down to rest at the top of a roadside elm. He did not see me coming till I was almost below the tree. Then he gaped, and started in alarm, and flew back towards the pond. He still moved slowly and carefully, as though fearful of spilling something, gliding with wings drooped down in limp, ignoble curves. This heavy waterlogged flight was like a crow's, with the tips of the wings giving the air a light, quick touch at the end of the wings' deep oaring.

I found him huddled in the oak that overhangs the lane, between the pond and the ford. He did not move when I passed beneath him. With eyes closed, and drying feathers ruffled by the wind, he perched very upright and wooden, looking dingy and comatose, as though long-dead and rather moth-eaten. When I clapped my hands, he roused and flew down to the copse by the ford. Flushed from there, he flew back to the oak. Three times this manœuvre was repeated. Then I left him to rest in the oak while I watched from the edge of the copse. He slept for another hour, waking at one o'clock to preen and look around. The colour of his feathers lightened as they dried. The tail was narrowly barred with pale fawn and pale brown; the back, mantle, and scapulars, were pale yellowish brown, flecked and barred laterally with glowing burnt sienna. The bars were close and narrow, and the whole surface had a luminous red-gold sheen. The crown of his head was pale gold, flecked lightly with brown. The tips of the folded wings reached just beyond the end of the tail; exceptionally long, even for a tiercel peregrine.

He left the tree at half past one, but was immediately chased back there by a crow. He called loudly in flight: a shrill, petulant sound. When perched, he called again: a deeper, more challenging cry. At two o'clock he became restless, moving his head up and down and shifting his feet about. He took several minutes to bring himself to it, but when he finally flew he was fast and decisive. He swung out and round in a rising arc and went steeply up over North Wood, striking the air smartly with his wings; earlier, he had merely stroked it. Jackdaws, that all day had been playing and feeding unconcernedly in pastures by the brook, now flew up in panic, circled high, and dispersed hastily.

Rain fell for an hour, but I stayed by the copse, waiting. At three o'clock the peregrine returned, flying fast and savagely into the cold north wind, throwing up gulls and lapwings. A lapwing was cut off from the flock, and the lean brown tiercel cleaved behind, low to the ground as a running hare. The two birds seemed to be looped together, then seemed to swing apart. The lapwing turned in its own length, but the hawk wheeled out on a wider arc and whipped back in again with frenzied wings. Suddenly the tethering cord was broken. The hawk rushed up into the sky, the lapwing tumbled forward. The hawk turned on its side and stooped, as though hurled down through a hole in the air. Then nothing. Nothing at all. However it had ended, it was over. There was only silence and the hissing of the wind. The tortuous coiling of the hunter and his victim seemed to hang in the gloomy air.

As I went up the lane from the ford I saw a bird's wing fluttering in the grey-twigged crown of a pollard ash. When I was two yards away, the peregrine flew out, his wings drumming in a frantic effort to wrench himself clear. For a second he was very close, and I could see the satin smoothness of his underwings and the thickly quilted feathers, spotted with brown and cream. He flew south across the fields, veering and swaying erratically. His legs hung down, and there was something white between them that fluttered like paper. Through binoculars I saw that he was carrying the dead lapwing, gripping it with both feet, so that it lay up against his tail, breast upward and head foremost, with its wings lolling open to show their black and white undersides. He flew easily, carrying his half-pound load, but he was troubled by the strength of the wind. He sagged a little in the gusts, and his wings beat in quick short jabs. He landed in a tree near the lane. When I disturbed him, five minutes later, the lapwing was smaller and easier to carry. He flew into another pollard ash, and there I left him to finish his meal. Three tractors were still ploughing in the field beside him.

At sunset, ten curlew rose and flew east, calling loudly. The tractors went back to the farm, and the last gulls flew south. The peregrine circled high in the dusk, and flickered out into the darkness of the hill. The hawkless valley bloomed with the soft voices of the waking owls.

December 15th. The warm west gale heaved and thundered across the flat river plain, crashed and threshed high its crests of airy spray against the black breakwater of the wooded ridge. The stark horizon, fringing the far edges of the wind, was still and silent. Its clear serenity moved back before me; a mirage of elms and oaks and cedars, farms and houses, churches, and pylons silver-webbed like swords.

At eleven o'clock the tiercel peregrine flew steeply up above the river, arching and shrugging his wings into the gale, dark on the grey clouds racing over. Wild peregrines love the wind, as otters love water. It is their element. Only within it do they truly live. All wild peregrines I have seen have flown longer and higher and further in a gale than at any other time. They avoid it only when bathing or sleeping. The tiercel glided at two hundred feet, spread his wings and tail upon the billowing air, and turned down wind in a long and sweeping curve. Quickly his circles stretched away to the east, blown out elliptically by the force of the wind. Hundreds of birds rose beneath him. The most exciting thing about a hawk is the way in which it can create life from the still earth by conjuring flocks of birds into the air. All the feeding gulls and lapwings and woodpigeons went up from the big field between the road and the brook as the hawk circled above them. The farm seemed to be hidden by a sheet of white water, so close together were the rising gulls. Dark through the white gulls the sharp hawk dropped, shattering them apart like flinging white foam. When I lowered my binoculars, I saw that the birds around me had also been watching the hawk. In bushes and trees there were many sparrows, starlings, blackbirds and thrushes, looking east and steadily chattering and scolding. And all the way along the lanes, as I hurried east, there were huddles of small birds lining the hedges, shrilling their warning to the empty sky.

As I passed the farm, a flock of golden plover went up like a puff of gunsmoke. The whole flock streamed low, then slowly rose, like a single golden wing. When I reached ford lane, the trees by the pond were full of woodpigeons. None moved when I walked past them, but from the last tree of the line the peregrine flew up into the wind and circled east. The pigeons immediately left the trees, where they had been comparatively safe, and flew towards North Wood. They passed below the peregrine. He could have stooped at them if he had wished to do so. Woodpigeons are very fast and wary, but like teal they sometimes have a fatal weakness for flying towards danger instead of away from it.

In long arcs and tangents the hawk drifted slowly higher. From five hundred feet above the brook, without warning, he suddenly fell. He simply stopped, flung his wings up, dived vertically down. He seemed to split in two, his body shooting off like an arrow from the tight-strung bow of his wings. There was an unholy impetus in his falling, as though he had been hurled from the sky. It was hard to believe, afterwards, that it had happened at all. The best stoops are always like that, and they often miss. A few seconds later the hawk flew up from the brook and resumed his eastward circling, moving higher over the dark woods and orchards till he was lost to sight. I searched the fields, but found no kill. Woodpigeons in hawthorns, and snipe in the marshy ground, were tamed by their greater fear of the hawk. They did not fly when I went near them. Partridges crouched together in the longest grass.

Rain began, and the peregrine returned to the brook. He

flew from an elm near the bridge, and I lost him at once in the hiss and shine of rain and the wet shuddering of the wind. He looked thin and keen, and very wild. When the rain stopped, the wind roared into frenzy. It was hard to stand still in the open, and I kept to the lee of the trees. At half past two the peregrine swung up into the eastern sky. He climbed vertically upward, like a salmon leaping in the great waves of air that broke against the cliff of South Wood. He dived to the trough of a wave, then rose steeply within it, flinging himself high in the air, on outstretched wings exultant. At five hundred feet he hung still, tail closed, wings curving far back with their tips almost touching the tip of his tail. He was stooping horizontally forward at the speed of the oncoming wind. He rocked and swayed and shuddered, close-hauled in a roaring sea of air, his furled wings whipping and plying like wet canvas. Suddenly he plunged to the north, curved over to the vertical stoop, flourished his wings high, shrank small, and fell.

He fell so fast, he fired so furiously from the sky to the dark wood below, that his black shape dimmed to grey air, hidden in a shining cloud of speed. He drew the sky about him as he fell. It was final. It was death. There was nothing more. There could be nothing more. Dusk came early. Through the almost dark, the fearful pigeons flew quietly down to roost above the feathered bloodstain in the woodland ride.

December 17th. The low sun was dazzling, the south a polar blaze. The north wind was cold. The night's frost was un-melted, white on the grass like salt, and crisp in the morning sun.

The falcon peregrine flew tentatively up wind, and hovered over the still, white fields. The air would not be warm enough for soaring for another hour at least; till then, she was simply passing the time. Her hovering was desultory. She moved idly from tree to tree. You can almost feel the boredom of a hawk that has bathed and preened and is neither hungry nor sleepy. It seems to lounge about, stirring up trouble, just for the sake of something to do.

The morning was strange and wraith-like, very pure and new. The frosted fields were quiet. The sun had no grip of warmth. Where the frost had gone, the dry grass smelt of hay. Golden plover were close, softly calling. A corn bunting sang. The north wind brittled icily in the pleached lattice of the hedges, and smote through the thorny gaps. A woodcock swished up from the darkness of a ditch into the stinging gleam of light. It flew north with deep, sharp wing-beats, then looser, shallower ones. The falcon went after it, in a leisurely disinterested way. She did not come back, so I went down to the river.

At midday she rose from the willows and floated up into the wind, gliding briefly, or moving the tips of her wings in small paddling circles. They quivered rapidly, as though they were merely vibrating in the wind. The growing warmth of the sun had told her she could soar. She was delicately feeling her way forward till she found the first rising of the warmer air. Over the dead oak she glided very slowly, then spread out her wings and tail, and turned down wind. In wide sweeping arcs she drifted to the south, circling a hundred feet above me. Her long, powerful head, like a hooked pike glaring from reeds, flexed slowly round as she scanned the fields below. The two deep-brown moustachial bars shone glossily in the sun, hanging down each side of the bill like strips of polished leather. The large dark eyes, and the bare white patches of skin in front of them, glinted black and white like wet flint. The low sun glowed the hawk's colours into rich relief: copper and rust of dead beech leaves, shining damp-earth brown. She was a large and broad-winged hawk, a falcon unmistakably, spreading her long wings like a buzzard to win lift from the warm air rising from melting frost and from fields now steaming in the sun. I could almost hear the hiss and rustle of the parting air as she swished round in her taut muscular gliding.

Quickly she circled southward, turning in smaller arcs. I was afraid I would lose her in sun-dazzle, but she rose above it. She was moving faster, beating her wings between short glides, changing direction erratically. Sometimes she circled to left and right alternately, sometimes she went round clock-wise. When circling alternately, she looked intently inwards or down; when she went round in the same direction, she looked outwards or straight ahead. She leaned round in steep banking curves. Over the roofs of farm buildings warm air was rising faster. Thrusting her wings in quick pumping movements, and gliding at steep upward angles, the hawk climbed to a thousand feet, and drifted south-east. Then her circling stopped. She floated on the white surface of the sky. Half-way to the woods she circled up as before, adding another five hundred feet to her height, till she was almost hidden in mist and distance. Suddenly she glided to the north, cutting away very fast, occasionally beating her wings in a flurry. She flew a mile in much less than a minute, sweeping down through the sky from South Wood to the river, following the line of the brook, till she pierced the horizon in a puff of white gulls. Throughout this long flight, over three miles of valley, she rose so far and fast that perspective did not level her down to earth, in spite of the distance covered. I saw her only against the sky. To trace her movements I had always to lower the binoculars through thirty to forty degrees to pick out the landmarks beneath. She was wholly of the sun and wind and the purity of sky.

Birds were still restless when I reached the place where she had descended. Gulls circled along the rim of the valley; lapwings flew over from the east. Remote as a star, the falcon glided out towards the estuary, a purple speck kindling and fading through the frost-fire of the sky.

December 18th. The silent east wind breathed white frost on to grass and trees and the edges of still water, and the sun did not melt it. The sun shone from a cobalt sky that curved down, through pale violet, to cold and white horizons.

The reservoir glittered in the sun, still as ice, and rippling with duck. Ten goosander launched upward from the water in crystal troughs of foam, and rose superbly through the sky. All were drakes. Their long red bills, sleek green heads, and narrow straining necks, led their heavy, lean, bomb-shaped bodies forward under the black and white flicking fins of their wings. They were splendid imperial duck, regal in the long reaches of the sky.

The harsh whistling of goldeneyes' wings sounded constantly over the still water. When they were not flying, the drakes called 'ung-ick' through their noses—a thin, rasping sound—and shook their heavy-jowled dark heads so that their yellow-ringed eyes winked madly in the sun. Coot huddled together like winkles on a plate. Drake smew, their phantom arctic whiteness piped and curled about with thin black veins, sank deep like ice-floes or dazzled up the sky like flying snow.

I did not see a peregrine, though one was never far away. I found a black-headed gull that had been killed in the morning; it was still damp and bloody. Only the head, wings, and legs, were untouched. All other bones had been carefully stripped of flesh. What was left smelt fresh and sweet, like a mash of raw beef and pineapple. It was an appetising smell, not the least bit rank or fishy. I could have eaten it myself if I had been hungry.

December 20th. Mist cleared in the afternoon and widening rings of sunlight rippled out. A heron flew to a tree beside the brook. His legs reached down with a slow pedalling movement, like a man descending through the trap-door of a loft and feeling for a ladder with his feet. He touched the topmost twig, fumbled his spidery toes around it, gradually deflated himself down on to the long stilts of his legs, hunched and crumpling like a broken parasol.

Little owls called as I walked beside South Wood. The air was quiet. Birds were feeding in fields where frost had melted. Song thrushes bounced and sprang to spear out the surfacing worms. There is something very cold about a thrush, endlessly listening and stabbing through the arras of grass, the fixed eye blind to what it does. A cock blackbird, yellow-billed, stared with bulging crocus eye, like a small mad puritan with a banana in his mouth. I went into the wood

Dead leaves are crisp with frost. The silence is fretted with the whisper and lisp of tits feeding in the high branches. A goldcrest comes close, a tiny flicker of green in the dark wood, tonsured with a sliver of gold leaf. Its eyes shine large and bright, scanning each twig carefully before deciding which way to jump. It is never still as it deftly dabs up insects. When it is close, the thin ice-needles of its call ring out with surprising vehemence, but they are soon inaudible when it moves away. A pheasant rises suddenly from bracken, rocketing away between the tree-tops as though tight-wound elastic were shuddering loose inside a drum.

Light shines in woodland hollows, like still water. Birch twigs are a winish haze. A cock brambling calls, a grating nasal 'eez-eet,' bobbing and flicking his tail. His underparts are orange and white; glowing orange, like a sunset on silver scales of birch bark. A bounding flight of redpolls ripple out their harsh and tangy trills, hang upside down, dib deep into birch buds, then bound away. A redwing flits through the trees. Straw-coloured eye-stripes make its eyes look slanted. Its red wing-patches are like smeared blood.

Woodpigeons, gluttonous innocents, rise like grey breath from every frozen plough. They come early to roost, flushed by low sunlight to slow-burning gold that fades to purple as they descend into the tops of trees. Now their colour is like the mauve rim of a clear sky where the sun has just gone down. Hawks follow pigeon flocks as Red Indians once followed buffalo herds and as lions follow zebra. Woodpigeons are hawks' cattle.

Mallard fly along the line of the wood towards the lake. Looking up at them through binoculars, I see for the first time a falcon peregrine circling very high, beating and gliding in the fading light. She stoops, dilates like the pupil of an eye as it passes from day's brilliance into dusk. She is the size of a lark, then of a jay, now of a crow, now of a mallard. Mallard spray outwards and climb as she dives between them. She bends up through the sky again, curves under and up with the momentum of her stoop, crashes into a mallard, bursts it into a drift of feathers. Grappled together, they glide above the wood, then sweep down to the frosted ride. Mallard fly along the line of the wood towards the lake. Nothing has changed, though one is gone.

High on the steep slope of the hill, fieldfares are flying to roost. It is nearly dark. The tall, grizzled pines have a bony serenity. They tower against the skyline of the hill. It seems that beyond them there must be canyons and mist and nothing more. Silence hangs from their branches. The air tastes cold and metallic. The tiercel glides up to the trees, like a shadow. He calls once: a sound as final as the clanging of a portcullis. The glaring eyes squint up, and are sheathed in sleep. The hawk puffs out his feathers, looking cuddly and harmless. Only the armour-plated legs and the sickled toes do not relax, will never relax in life.

December 21st. Woodpigeons clouded the big fields between

river and brook, and a hundred mallard lifted through wheeling lapwings and gulls. Somewhere in the hissing, weaving smoke of wings curlew were calling and fading. The tiercel peregrine soared eastward in a calm, clear sky. Fog drifted slowly down from the sun.

Trees by the brook were grey with a lichen of woodpigeons. None flew for an hour; some stayed for much longer. All the trees to north and south were thick with them, they lined the hedges, they clustered heavily in the orchards on the hillside, the rising woods beyond—right up to the skyline ridge—were grey and distorted with them. Only a very deadly hawk could sweep three thousand woodpigeons out of the fields simply by soaring above them, and could keep them there for an hour, too fearful to fly.

I waited at the bridge. Birds were silent, and there was no wind. The sun shone in mist, like a burning moon. I hid in my own stillness. After one o'clock the sky became clearer, and the wind rose from the north. Lapwings skimmed over the top of South Wood and flew low across the fields. It was time to go on. I went up the hill, scanning the trees for a hawk. Wide pastures slope down to the upper part of South Wood, and on the far side there is a single small oak. A branch near the top had a slightly unnatural bulge. In binoculars this bulge grew into a peregrine, resting in the rounded, disarming, huddled-up shape of an owl. The mist had gone. The wind was blowing forward the first small fleeces of cloud. The hawk looked up at the sky and the cold, clear afternoon light. At this time of a winter's day one can see the light turn and begin to flake and burn down to the west in a cold mercurial glow. There is suddenly a feeling of 'too late,' which I am sure the hawk shares. After much stretching of wings and flexing of legs he flew from the tree at a quarter to two, wings lashing high, head reaching eagerly forward.

Above farm buildings he found warm air, and began to

rise. For twenty minutes I watched him hunting over the narrow wooded valleys and the hill beyond. He moved in a complex pattern of small intersecting circles, like chain-link fencing, threading alternately left and right. For one-third of each circle his wings beat sharply and deeply, with a definite bouncing rhythm. Then they flicked smartly down to a rigid line, and he glided round with stiff wings slowly rising. At the close of the circle they were high above his back and ready to begin beating again. Gliding was faster than beating. The whole turn of the circle was beautifully smooth.

At eight hundred feet his climbing ceased. The same even movements continued, as he carefully quartered the valley. Jackdaws and pigeons flew up, but there was no real panic. Blackbirds in the orchard behind me scolded for half an hour. South of the wood, where there is sloping ground out of the wind and flat to the sun's low angle, the hawk suddenly rose higher, lengthened his glides, and swept round in wider circles. He drifted southward, a thousand feet up, gliding slowly down wind. Over open parkland he found another thermal and circled within it till he was very high and small. From a great height he slanted gently down above the common, falling slowly to the skyline. Then he rose once more in a steep, flickering helix, hypnotic in style and rhythm, his long wings tireless and unfaltering. He shimmered and coiled and dwindled away over the sharp-spired hill, and was descending beyond it when distance suddenly quenched him. He left the blue sky baroque with fading curves of power and precision, of lithe and muscular flight.

December 22nd. The shortest day: dull, cold, with a sudden flare of sunlight before dusk. There were kills by the brook: curlew, lapwing, woodpigeon, jackdaw, and two black-headed gulls. At one o'clock the tiercel stooped again and again at a nimbly dodging gull. He descended the north slope of the hill in a series of abortive, rushing 'J's,' and I did not see him again.

Till long after sunset I waited on the hillside, thinking of peregrines. Few winter in England now, fewer nest here. Ten years ago, even five years, it was very different. Peregrines were seen almost every winter then: on the North Kent Marshes, from Cliffe to Sheppey; in the Medway valley; over the chain of artificial lakes in the Colne valley, and on the sterile plain of Middlesex; along the Thames from London to Oxford, and beyond; over the Berkshire and Wiltshire downs; along the Chiltern escarpment; on the high Cotswolds, and in the deep valleys of the small Cotswold rivers; across the wide river plains of the Trent, the Nene, and the Ouse; over the fens, the dry Breckland, and around the shores of the Wash; along the east coast from Thames to Humber. These were the traditional wintering places, remembered and revisited by dynasties of peregrines, deserted now because there are no descendants, because the ancient eyries are dying, their lineage gone.

Due west, eighty miles from here, the land rises to the north of Oxford, and goes on rising. Slowly the hills unwind their long horizons, and the land surfs up into limestone and hangs like a frozen wave of green above the Severn plain. The uniqueness of Cotswold is in air and stone; it is something very cold and pure. I remember the peregrines of those winter hills. They perched on the undulating limestone walls that glimmered in the deepening dusk and shone long after all the fields were dark, as though deep within their honey-coloured stone a candled twilight slowly died. High and heraldic, peregrines watched from the beech-crests and saw the beech-burnt horizons ringing the winter sky, that immense Cotswold sky, drifted with vast flocks of plover like debris from the flying curve of earth. Cotswold is its own place, withdrawn, remote. It has its own light, and cold, and sky, and monarchy of cloud. It will not be meshed in words. I remember following a peregrine down into a river valley on just such a frosty day as this. The hills were cold; the gustless wind was unceasing, a gentle leaning of ice into the face. But when cycling down into the steep-sided valley, I descended into coldness I had never imagined possible. Layers of ice seemed to shatter across my frozen face. The air smelt of iron, hard and implacable. It was like going down through the cold green strata of the sea. I remember those winter days with affection and nostalgia, those frozen fields ablaze with warring hawks. It is sad that it should be so no longer.

Chalk cliffs of the South; sky like blue smoke fuming from the sun; a cold north-east gale blowing. But in the lee of the cliffs the air as hot and stifling as hot canvas. The wind rushed off the land and roared across the sea, shredding waves to foam. The sea was a cool green wall of water, streamed with emerald and viridian, glazed with rich veins of cobalt, dissolving far out to amethyst and purple haze. It was all green foam and regal colour and white waves hissing and plunging on the stony shore.

I scrambled over chalk boulders and slippery rocks, stumbled across stretches of firm, pristine, cool, wave-moulded sand. Jackdaws and herring gulls were noisy on the cliffs. The clear metallic song of a rock pipit drifted slowly down the cliff-face. The tide receded. The day grew hotter and more stifling; the gale boomed and shuddered out to sea, two hundred feet above. The white cliffs scorched and dazzled, reflecting heat and light. My eyes were sore from endlessly stubbing against the aching whiteness of the chalk. By three o'clock I had given up all hope of hawks. Then, from the last high bastion before the haven, a tiercel peregrine flowed coolly out to sea, glided and soared down wind, till hidden in the bright sea haze. I went closer to the cliff. The falcon flew from a ledge near the top, and soared towards the tiercel. Together they rose and faded in the distant sky.

I saw them many times in the days that followed. They had a nest-scrape, but no eggs or young. They spent the day just sitting on the cliff or soaring out to sea. Their hunting was done inland, very early and late, and it did not take long. They seemed bored, sterile; they had no meaning.

Above, they were the colour of the sea's deepest blue; below, like the soiled whiteness of shadowed chalk. In the turbulent air above the cliffs and shallows they soared for hours, hoping perhaps to lure away intruders from their nesting place. Invisible even in a telescope magnifying sixty times, even in the purest summer sky, they drifted idly above the glittering Channel water. They had no song. Their calls were harsh and ugly. But their soaring was like an endless silent singing. What else had they to do? They were sea falcons now; there was nothing to keep them to the land. Foul poison burned within them like a burrowing fuse. Their life was lonely death, and would not be renewed. All they could do was take their glory to the sky. They were the last of their race.

December 23rd. Bright frosty day, fading from brightness slowly, hour by hour. Jack snipe waver up from the still edges of a pond tall with tufted reeds and rimmed with dark ice. They call faintly, dodge feebly, rise with a hesitant stutter of wing-beats, drop carelessly to cover as though too weak to fly farther. I cannot flush them again. Snipe flare up and are gone. Jack snipe burn slowly, flicker, then slowly fade.

A green sandpiper towers from the brook, fluttering low overhead: stiff-winged, jerky, erratic as a dragonfly, white breast shining between black wings. Thrush-size, narrow and frail-looking, it spurts away like a jumping cracker. It always flies in this jagged way. The darting and dodging is not due to fear; it is just its natural style.

North Wood is quiet. I watch a treecreeper feeding. His bent bill is as cruel-looking as a hawk's, a thin talon, a dangerous thorn. He climbs on the surface of a tree, then slants down to the bottom of another, transecting the wood from east to west, never missing a tree, never scanning the same tree twice. Only when you follow him for a long time can you realise how systematic he is. He may pass several trees by, but he will always go back to them. He straddles on to the bark, big spidery feet placed wide apart, and moves upward in frog-like jerks, picking and carving out insects from crevices lit by his shining egg-white breast. His bill is designed for delicate probing, but he can also dig and hammer with it, and can catch insects with it as he flies. He hunts by eye and ear, peering closely at the bark, or listening to it with his head inclined. As he climbs he may press his tail against the tree for support, but this is not done invariably; often there is a gap of an inch or two between tail and tree. He can walk sideways, or head-downwards, like a nuthatch. Where a tree branches out, he hesitates, squinting along the surface of each branch in turn before choosing his way. His high thin call comes piercingly from wide-open bill. His underparts are white, tinged here and there with green, like a freshly peeled onion. The markings on his folded wings look like faded moths. Like the bark of a tree, they are a blend of grey and brown and fawn, striated to the light and shade of wood's ridge and fissure. He silvers in sunlight, like a glistening water shrew. Like a shrew, he hides in stillness when a kestrel passes over.

Light moves out to the fringes of the wood and across the evening fields. A tawny owl calls from the wood's dark hornbeam heart. He gives a vibrant groan; a long sensitive pause is held till almost unbearable; then he looses the strung bubbles of his tremulous hollow song. It echoes down to the brook, breaking the frozen surface of the air. I look out at the west's complexity of light. A heron, black against the yellow sky, kinked neck and dagger bill incised, sweeps silently down into the brook's dark gulf. The sky infuses with the afterglow.

Softly through the dusk the peregrine glides, hushing it aside with silent wings. He searches the constellations of small eyes, sees the woodcock's planetary eye look upward from the marsh, shafts back his wings, and plunges to the light. The woodcock rises, twists under the blade of the hawk, and wavers away. He is overtaken, cut down. He drops with a squelching thud. The hawk lands on the softening bird, grips its neck in his bill. I hear the bone snap, like barbed wire cut by pliers. He nudges the dead bird over. Its wings wave, then it lies on its back. I hear the tearing of feathers, the tug of flesh, the crack and snap of gristle. I can see the black blood dripping from the gleam of the hawk's bill. I move out of the dark of the wood into the paler shadows of trees. The hawk hears, looks up. His white-ringed eyes are huge with dusk. I creep nearer, knees soaking in the marshy ground. Thin ice crunches. Frost is forming where the late sun shone. The hawk pulls at his prey, looks up. Four yards separate us, but it is too far, a distance as unspannable as a thousand foot crevasse. I drag like a wounded bird, floundering, sprawled. He watches me, moving his head, looking with each eye in turn. An otter whistles. Something splashes in the cold, piky depth of the brook. The hawk is poised now on the narrow edge between curiosity and fear. What is he thinking? Is he thinking at all? This is new to him. He does not know how I got here. Slowly I mask the pallor of my face. He is not afraid. He is watching the white glitter of my eyes. He cannot understand their staccato flicker. If I could stop them moving he would stay. But I cannot stop them. There is a breath of wings. He has flown into the trees. The owl calls. I stand above the kill. Red ice reflects the stars.

December 24th. The day hardened in the easterly gale, like a flawless crystal. Columns of sunlight floated on the land. The unrelenting clarity of the air was solid, resonant, cold and pure and remote as the face of the dead.

Near the brook a heron lay in frozen stubble. Its wings were stuck to the ground by frost, and the mandibles of its bill were frozen together. Its eyes were open and living, the rest of it was dead. All was dead but the fear of man. As I approached I could see its whole body craving into flight. But it could not fly. I gave it peace, and saw the agonised sunlight of its eyes slowly heal with cloud.

No pain, no death, is more terrible to a wild creature than its fear of man. A red-throated diver, sodden and obscene with oil, able to move only its head, will push itself out from the sea-wall with its bill if you reach down to it as it floats like a log in the tide. A poisoned crow, gaping and helplessly floundering in the grass, bright yellow foam bubbling from its throat, will dash itself up again and again on to the descending wall of air, if you try to catch it. A rabbit, inflated and foul with myxomatosis, just a twitching pulse beating in a bladder of bones and fur, will feel the vibration of your footstep and will look for you with bulging, sightless eyes. Then it will drag itself away into a bush, trembling with fear.

We are the killers. We stink of death. We carry it with us. It sticks to us like frost. We cannot tear it away.

At midday the peregrine soared above the hill, and lapwings wheeled and flowed across the sky. They had come in from the south-east on morning migration, and the hawk had risen to meet them. He stooped. A woodpigeon dropped from the sky as though dead, spread his wings, and landed with a thud in a spurt of frosty earth. He stayed there for ten minutes, looking up, with his bill gaping open. He glowed purple and grey like broccoli, in the white field.

I went down into the deep gulley of the narrow wood. Ashes and hornbeams filtered the sun's glare. Many birds were feeding on steep slopes where the frost had melted. Woodcock ripped away from brambles by the stream. There was a faint panting of wings. A small cloud of dusk flickered across the barred sunlight, like the shadow of something higher. Thirty yards away from me, across the thickness of the wood, it swooped up to perch on the branch of an oak. It was a sparrowhawk. The joy of such a moment can be relished for life, though the colour of the memory will slowly fade, like the plumage of a stuffed bird in a glass case. Looking through the telescope, my eye seemed amazingly close to the small head of the hawk. It is a head rather similar in proportion to that of a partridge or chicken; rounded at the crown, with the feathers sleeking up to a slight peak at the back. The curved bill, going down and under, looked as though it had been pushed deep into the face. The grey and brown feathers were streaked and mottled with fawn; good camouflage against the bark of trees or the dappled canopy of sunlit leaves. After landing, it crouched slightly forward, stretching its neck and looking around. Its head flicked from side to side quickly and flexibly, darting and jerking. The eyes were large in relation to the slender, rather flattened head. They had small dark pupils surrounded by a wide yellow iris. They were a blazing blankness, an utterly terrifying insanity of searing yellow, raging and seething like sulphurous craters. They seemed to shine in the dimness like jellies of yellow blood.

The glaring madness died away. The hawk unstiffened, and began to preen. Then its eyes kindled again. It swooped softly down from its perch, and flitted away to the east. It rose and fell, following the contour of the ground, keeping just above the hornbeam coppice, twisting between the tall oak standards. It did not glide. It beat its wings quickly, deeply, and very quietly, like an owl, flicking the air lightly with the splayed tips of its primaries. Woodpigeons feeding on acorns or hazel nuts do not see the sparrowhawk till it is pouncing down upon them from a tree. They struggle, but they are unarmed matronly creatures and cannot combat the hawk's cruel spurs. They are ridden to the ground and are executed there by the riving bill.

The sparrowhawk lurks in dusk; in true dusk, in the dusk before dawn, in the dusty cobwebby dusk of hazel and hornbeam, in the thick gloomy dusk of firs and larches. It will fold into a tree as though it had been thrown there, reminding me of the sticks I used to throw into chestnut trees to dislodge conkers. Suddenly a stick would wedge in a branch and be lost, and nothing could be done about it. The sparrowhawk can be like that: you see it fly in, but you do not see it go. You have lost it.

I came out of the wood at three o'clock to find the peregrine circling west above the brook. His back and wing-coverts shone in the sun as though they were covered with hard overlapping scales of chitin. They gleamed between the dark blue-black primaries, like red and gold chain-mail.

Cold air rises from the ground as the sun goes down. The eye-burning clarity of the light intensifies. The southern rim of the sky glows to a deeper blue, to pale violet, to purple, then thins to grey. Slowly the wind falls, and the still air begins to freeze. The solid eastern ridge is black; it has a bloom on it like the dust on the skin of a grape. The west flares briefly. The long, cold amber of the afterglow casts clear black lunar shadows. There is an animal mystery in the light that sets upon the fields like a frozen muscle that will flex and wake at sunrise. I feel compelled to lie down in this numbing density of silence, to companion and comfort the dying in these cold depths at the foot of the solstice: those that have fled from the falcon in the sky, from the hawk in the dark of the wood, from the foxes, stoats, and weasels, now running over the frozen fields, from the otter swimming in the icy brook; those whose blood now courses from the hunting frost, whose frail hearts choke in the clawed frost's bitter grip.

December 27th. Snow lay thick in South Wood, making the trees look black and hard, muffling the small sounds of the birds. Twigs rattled in the wind, fretting across mysteries of light. The call of a sparrowhawk shrilled out its alarm. It was a high nasal chatter, a fast cat-thin skirling, like a speeded-up recording of the song of a nightjar, rising and falling, slowly slurring and fading, ebbing and whimpering away to silence.

The sparrowhawk came softly from the trees, flicking aside faint dusts of snow. He swept into the open ride. Where it dipped to the stream there was a sheltered slope. The sun had melted the snow there, and many birds were feeding among dead leaves. As all the birds rose, the tiercel peregrine dived from a high tree. He hit nothing. The sparrowhawk flew on, apparently not recognising his danger. The peregrine turned and rushed at him. The hawk tore at the air with his wings, forced himself away into the cover of the trees. The peregrine followed him. The stillness of the hornbeams suddenly pulsed with a fierce panting of wings. The peregrine kept to the wider spaces between the tree-tops, the hawk weaved through thicker, lower growth. The peregrine was faster, the hawk more agile. When the hawk perched, the peregrine did the same. They glared at each other in the snow-lit gloom, the orange-ringed eyes of the sparrowhawk looking up at the peregrine's sombre white-ringed brown. The hawk's eyes glowed like points of distant fire. Rapt in their curious conflict they did not notice me at all.

For ten minutes the even chase endured, in endless rushing

circuits through thorn and ash and hornbeam. The peregrine would not risk a stoop in such a narrow space, the sparrow-hawk was safe if he kept in cover. But he did not know he was safe. He could not feel safe while the peregrine was still above him. Suddenly he dashed out of the wood and across the open fields. The peregrine flew down at him from tree-top height, caught him before he had gone a hundred yards, carried him down to the surface of the snow.

I saw him afterwards. He had been an adult male. His grey wings lay like flakes of beech bark beside the peeled willow of his shining yellow bones and the sunset feathers of his tigered breast.

December 29th. The fields were covered by three inches of snow, glittering in the powerless morning sun. Many birds have gone, or have been silenced by the cold. There was no ease or comfort in the bleak, tense air.

A jackdaw hopped from branch to branch of a tree by the valley road, endlessly calling 'chak, chak,' a hard brittle sound like the smack of wood on wood, which meant it had seen a hawk. As I went down the snow-drifted path to the brook the tiercel peregrine flew towards me from a tree near the bridge. He passed overhead, looking sideways and down. For the first time, I realised that he may watch for my arrival in the valley. The predictability of my movements may have made him more curious, and more trusting. He may associate me now with the incessant disturbance of prey, as though I too were a species of hawk. The snow will make it difficult for me to keep as close to him as I have been.

White light shone up from the snow and reflected down from the breast of the hawk a pale golden radiance, in which the interlocking hackles of dark brown and fawn seemed to be deeply embedded. The crown of his head gleamed like a pale yellow crescent inlaid with ivory and gold. Two hundred crouching mallard were black smudges in the whiteness of the snow; woodpigeons and skylarks made smaller dots and blotches. The hawk looked down and saw them all, but he did not attack. He perched in a tree near the road, with his back towards me, huddled down in the shape of a swede or of a huge copper-coloured beetle. He did not see me approach, but his head turned when he heard the crunch of my boots. He went steadily eastwards, clearly imprinted on the whiteness of the snow and on the shining egg-white of the sky, but hidden at once in the black line of the woods.

This was the way he flew. The inner wings were held up at an angle of forty-five degrees to the body. They did not move far. They jerked forward a little as the outer wings swung back, and back slightly when the outer wings went forward. The outer wings flicked round with a quick sculling rhythm, flexible and willowy. No two wing-beats were identical. There was an endless variation in the depth, speed, and diameter, of their revolutions. One wing seemed occasionally to bite deeper than the other, causing the hawk to veer and tilt from side to side. Altitude was never constant; it was always slightly rising or falling. This bird has unusual power, and a strangely individual style; he glides and rocks away from each free swing forward and sweet pull backward of the long, tapering sculls of his wings.

I followed him east, but could not find him again. Snow clouds to the north were pale white above a counter-shading of deep blue-grey. They were very shiny and smooth-looking, and they never came any nearer. There was shooting all day in the woods, and at dusk every hedge was lined with guns. The woodpigeons have no food, no rest. Thousands fly north, thousands remain. A few feeble thrushes fed in ditches, thin-necked, with loose, pinched flanks. Two gaunt herons tottered in the shallows of the brook where water still moves freely. A wave of turquoise froze into a kingfisher standing on a stone, then broke, and flowed away round a bend of the stream.

I avoid humans, but hiding is difficult now the snow has come. A hare dashed away, with its ears laid back, pitifully large and conspicuous. I use what cover I can. It is like living in a foreign city during an insurrection. There is an endless banging of guns and tramping of feet in the snow. One has an unpleasantly hunted feeling. Or is it so unpleasant? I am as solitary now as the hawk I pursue.

January 5th. Broken columns of snow towered over lanes dug from ten-foot drifts. Roads were ridged and fanged with ice, opaque and shiny as frozen rivers. Goldfinches sparkled in snow-lit hedges. Gulls and crows patrolled the white beaches of the fields, looking for stranded corpses. Through mist, under low cloud, hundreds of woodpigeons flew north-east.

A blackbird scolding by the ford at midday was the first bird sound I heard. It stopped when the peregrine flew slowly north into the mist. Near the farm, two thousand wood-pigeons were feeding on brussels sprouts. Three or four birds clung to each stalk, while others fluttered round them or sat in the snow, waiting. The surrounding fields were black with resting pigeons. They hid the snow. Shots were fired, and many birds fell dead. The others roared into the sky. The white sky became black as the black ground whitened. A mile away, the sound of wings was like an aircraft taking off. At a hundred yards, it was unbelievably loud, a landslide of crashing reverberant clangour engulfing the banging of guns and the shouts of men. In woods and orchards there were thousands more of these desperate birds, and vast flocks flew over to the north and north-east, searching for an end to the whiteness below. They go down before the guns, like the cavalry at Balaclava. Rapt in their hunger, they have no guile left. Their bodies pile high at the farms. Their grey faces are weary, their eyes sodden with defeat.

Above the brook a kingfisher hovered. Its body seemed to be suspended between two shining silver spheres of water, so fast were its wings beating. It half dived, half fell, and its bill hit ice with a loud click like a bone breaking. It could see a fish below the ice, but it did not know what ice was. It lay on its belly, stunned or dead, sprawling like a brilliantly coloured toad. A minute later it skidded up into the air and flew feebly downstream.

There are a few short stretches of open water left, but they too will soon be frozen. Last summer, kingfishers nested in the bank of the stream that flows down to the brook through South Wood. The marshy ground below the tall thin trees shone with kingcups. Bluebells on the higher slopes were a blue mist above the yellow. The tremulous shrill song of a kingfisher—as though it were breathing deeply in and out as it whistled—descended towards me through the wood and along the windings of the stream. Suddenly the kingfisher appeared in front of me, hovered, and flew silently back. In the green sunlight dappled on the water it gleamed like a luminous-sharded rain beetle. It had a glow-worm radiance, as though it were under water and sheathed in a bubble of silver air. It clouded the sun's reflection with a streaming haze of emerald blue. Now it is slowly dying in the blind glare of the snow. Soon it will be sepulchred in the ice it cannot pierce, crushed into frozen light below the dark cave where it was born.

A fungus of whiteness grows upon the eye, and spreads along the nerves like pain.

January 9th. The sun shone today for the first time this year. It was the clearest, coldest day I have ever known. North of ford lane a heron stood knee-deep in snow. The gale did not rock him; his long grey feathers were unruffled. Regal and frozen and dead, he stood to the wind in his thin sarcophagus of ice. Already he seemed to be dynasties away from me. I have outlived him, as the gibbering ape outlived the dinosaur.

A feeble moorhen walked stealthily across the frozen brook, with hushed, arthritic tread; the gait of the dying, yet still pathetically funny to watch. Bud-feeding bullfinches coloured the white orchards. Woodcock dashed from ditches in flurries of loose snow.

At one o'clock a pipistrelle flittered above the lane, twisting and diving as though it were catching insects. None could be flying on so cold a day. Perhaps it had been roused by the sunlight, and was hunting in a dream of summer.

The white fields were littered with black rocks of birds; with the bulky outlines of mallard, moorhen, and partridge; with the narrower shapes of woodcock and pigeon; with the small spots and streaks of blackbirds, thrushes, finches, and larks. There is no concealment. It is easy now for hawks. Their eyes see maps of black and white, like a crackle of silent film. The moving black is prey.

The tiercel peregrine hurled down wind and rose on a gusting surge of birds. As the wave broke upward he stabbed down through the heart of it, so that the pulse died and the birds dropped back into the snow. A woodpigeon flew on with the hawk, limp and fluttering in the gin-trap of his foot, spilling red feathers and slow blood.

January 18th. Still, hazy, cloudless; the small sun pale and shrunken in a white sky. The frozen river cracked and whanged out into diamond shapes of ice. By dusk it had sealed into rigidity again. Some ponds were solid ice. They could be lifted up, leaving no water.

I saw the tiercel peregrine at three o'clock, on the far side of the river. He was hovering and plunging and darting over the snow in a strange manner, leaping with a wonderfully soft dancing lightness, like a big nightjar. Dark against the low sun, he flickered and danced in his own twilight, as erratic and darting as the green sandpiper I had seen by the river in the morning.

When I went closer, I saw the reason for his antics. He was chasing the enfeebled sandpiper till it was too tired to fly any farther. It jinked about below the hawk, flickering its wings stiffly back like the striding legs of a water beetle, like the prey it could not find.

Gradually its flight weakened, and it fluttered down into the snow, exhausted. The hawk pounced, plucked and ate it in five minutes, and flew off. The snow flamed redly in the last light of the sun, glowed orange, then faded to white again. The red embers of the kill shone into the dusk, pitting the snow with bright orange blood.

January 25th. Today I walked for ten miles beside the river. Horizons were misty, the sun cold with blue sky above, the north wind light. I trudged through dazzling foot-deep snow. Herring gulls in snow were calm as camels in the desert. They flew languidly up, moving reluctantly, slowly, like cattle making way. Their whiteness was made wraith-like, unsubstantial, by the white gleam of the snow. All the gulls were near towns; there was none in open country. Fifteen moorhens crowded into a ditch. Fieldfares flew to a willow, shaking snow from its branches. They were thin and drawn-looking, and their loud calls seemed too big for their shrunken frames. A pied wagtail danced on ice, tripping and slithering. Jackdaws and rooks fed near the farms, and were very tame. Little grebes swam in stretches of open water, diving when they saw me coming. They were like small brown coracles, fat-bottomed, and kettle-shaped.

Six hares crouched together under hawthorns in the middle

of a field. Three ran left, three right. Gunfire broke like bars of ice snapping. A peregrine flew over, hurtling away very fast, beating its wings in a low shimmer like a steep-rising teal. Willows were lined with woodpigeons, a frozen smoke of purple and grey. Six pheasants rattled up from a scrub-covered island. Two men were cutting and burning brambles, hacking fiercely with billhooks, smoke and breath twining away through the freezing blue air. A large snipe flew slowly across the river, and pitched into a hedge. Its white outer tail feathers spread and shone as it landed. It was probably a great snipe.

Skylarks, meadow pipits, reed buntings, and chaffinches, perched in riverside trees, feeble and dying. A wren crept over the sloping roof of a wooden church tower, sneaking up like a treecreeper, and went inside through a belfry slat. A moorhen plunged down through hawthorns, feet first, in a fizz and spray of powdery snow. Tangles of thistles pierced the even surface of the snow. Three goldfinches were feeding on thistle seeds, contorting their necks, dibbing out each separate seed with their bills. They fluttered and hovered over the thistle-heads, like flycatchers. Their calls chipped at the frosty air.

The low, afternoon sun shone upward to the southward flying gulls. They seemed to be almost transparent, ethereal with the glowing and holy illumination that hollowed out their slender bones and threaded their airy marrow.

Two dead herons lay in the snow together, like a pair of gaunt grey crutches; eyeless and tattered corpses, torn and shredded by many shapes of tooth and beak and claw. Otter tracks led to fish-blood and the bones of pike. A moorhen was dragged back and down under water by a pike that had lanced up at it through a hole in the ice; it tilted over and up and sank like a torpedoed ship.

I stood by a wooden barn, weighing a frozen and shrivelled

white owl in my hand. I had lifted it down from a rafter as though it had been a flower-pot. It was cold and dry and brittle, stale and long-dead. Something hit the roof of the barn, slithered down, and fell at my feet. It was a woodpigeon. Blood welled from its eye like a red tear, and spread over its face in a horrifying lop-sided circle. The other eye stared out, impelling the bird round in the snow. It clutched with its wings, half of its brain already dead. When I lifted it up, it still kept turning, turning, like a toy train that is meaningless away from its rails. I killed it, threw it down in the snow, and walked on. The chattering, circling peregrine descended to its prey.

The long, waning whiteness of the afternoon stained towards sunset. The sun was like a withered apple, shrivelling, dying. Dusk shaded the sliding hill lanes under spruces alpine with snow. Fieldfares and redwings, a few tired birds, went down into the dark valley, perhaps for the last time. A tawny owl's song, tremulously baying, rang out from holly and pine. Night. A fox calling, blazing up before me in the torch-lit snow, glaring from a grate of blood and pheasant feathers, red and copper shavings.

A day of blood; of sun, snow, and blood. Blood-red! What a useless adjective that is. Nothing is as beautifully, richly red as flowing blood on snow. It is strange that the eye can love what mind and body hate.

January 30th. Through the frosted window-pane at sunrise I saw bullfinches feeding in the apple trees, the bright fire of their breasts glowing, then the sullen red smoke of the sun breathing from the eastern rim.

Robins sang as the snow fell; otherwise there was silence, like a ring of steel round the head. A little owl scuttled out of a hedge and ran into the middle of the road, stopped, looked up at me, a scowling feathered face under fierce brows. It was like a glaring, severed head looking up from the snow-flecked road. Then the owl flew wildly back to the hedge, suddenly realising what he had done. It was a numbing day, leaden and cold.

Going downhill, I flashed past a barn. Stacks and loose straw moved up and over the eye in a sudden mass of yellow, like a cloud of shining hair. Sparrows were shrilling, disintegrating upward. The clutching grey slash of a sparrowhawk flicked across the eye like a twig lashing back. I had swooped round the bend of the road like a hawk swooping, startling both hawk and prey.

All the way to the coast there were sparrow and finch flocks at the farms, but few in between. A whirl of goldfinches hurled out of the snow into the warm smell of a barn, dancing lightly as snowflakes, chiming like rain on a tin roof.

Ice floes and shelduck gleamed on the grey sea, equally white and dazzling. The weak and hungry larks were very tame. Small birds fed in ditches or on the saltings, where tufts of vegetation still protruded from the snow. There was a bitter silence, a slow dying. Everything sank down to the frozen edge of the grey lunar sea.

February 10th. This was a day made absolute, the sun unflawed, the blue sky pure. Slate roofs and crows' wings burned white like magnesium. The shining mauve and silver woods, snow-rooted, bit sharply black into the solid blueness of the sky. The air was cold. The wind rose from the north, like cold fire. All was revealed, the moment of creation, a rainbow poured upon rock and shaped into woods and rivers.

The peregrine flew north across the valley. He was half a mile away, but I could see the brown and black of his wings, the shining gold of his back. The pale cream of his tail coverts looked like a band of straw twined round the base of his tail. Thinking he would return down wind, I went into the fields by the river to watch for him. I stood in the lee of a hawthorn hedge, looking through it to the north, sheltered from the bitter wind. By midday, small cumulus clouds were smoking up from the horizon. They were very white, but those that followed were greyer and larger. Warm air was rising where snow had thawed.

The hawk must have circled over, high and unseen, for at one o'clock he was moving up wind again across the open fields. Already he was two hundred feet up, and climbing fast. He sculled easily forward, then glided. With every glide he lifted fifty feet into the wind. At five hundred feet he spread his wings and tail and turned away in slow majestic arcs. Each long luxuriant circle floated him a hundred feet higher, and the wind drifted him southward. In half a minute he had doubled his height and was very small, and far beyond the river; another half-minute and he was barely visible, two thousand feet above the fields. The thermal tower of air, which had wafted him so high, cooled away in the wind. He began to beat his wings rapidly between glides, moving in narrower circles. Joy became hunting. He was quick and nimble in the sky, intricately weaving and threading the loops of his figures of eight. His wings sprang sharply back from the resilient air. He crossed the sun and was hidden, but I found him on the other side, climbing higher and smaller. A blackbird in the hedge behind me must suddenly have seen him for the first time. In spite of the great distance between them he started to scold frantically, jumping from twig to twig in an agony of apprehension. The hawk became very small. I thought he must be leaving for the coast, but when almost out of sight he swung round in a glide and came down and back into the wind, till I could just see the shape of his wings. In light less perfect I would never have seen him at all, for I was looking up, at a sixty degree angle, at a bird half a mile away.

He hovered, and stayed still, striding on the crumbling columns of air, curved wings jerking and flexing. Five minutes he stayed there, fixed like a barb in the blue flesh of sky. His body was still and rigid, his head turned from side to side, his tail fanned open and shut, his wings whipped and shuddered like canvas in the lash of the wind. He side-slipped to his left, paused, then glided round and down into what could only be the beginning of a tremendous stoop. There is no mistaking the menace of that first easy drifting fall. Smoothly, at an angle of fifty degrees, he descended; not slowly, but controlling his speed; gracefully, beautifully balanced. There was no abrupt change. The angle of his fall became gradually steeper till there was no angle left, but only a perfect arc. He curved over and slowly revolved, as though for delight, glorying in anticipation of the dive to come. His feet opened and gleamed golden, clutching up towards the sun. He rolled over, and they dulled, and turned towards the ground beneath, and closed again. For a thousand feet he fell, and curved, and slowly turned, and tilted upright. Then his speed increased, and he dropped vertically down. He had another thousand feet to fall, but now he fell sheer, shimmering down through dazzling sunlight, heart-shaped, like a heart in flames. He became smaller and darker, diving down from the sun. The partridge in the snow beneath looked up at the black heart dilating down upon him, and heard a hiss of wings rising to a roar. In ten seconds the hawk was down, and the whole splendid fabric, the arched reredos and immense fan-vaulting of his flight, was consumed and lost in the fiery maelstrom of the sky.

And for the partridge there was the sun suddenly shut out, the foul flailing blackness spreading wings above, the roar ceasing, the blazing knives driving in, the terrible white face descending—hooked and masked and horned and staring-eyed. And then the back-breaking agony beginning, and snow scattering from scuffling feet, and snow filling the bill's wide silent scream, till the merciful needle of the hawk's beak notched in the straining neck and jerked the shuddering life away.

And for the hawk, resting now on the soft flaccid bulk of his prey, there was the rip and tear of choking feathers, and hot blood dripping from the hook of the beak, and rage dying slowly to a small hard core within.

And for the watcher, sheltered for centuries from such hunger and such rage, such agony and such fear, there is the memory of that sabring fall from the sky, and the vicarious joy of the guiltless hunter who kills only through his familiar, and wills him to be fed.

February 17th. The crests of the higher fields are dappled brown and white, but snow is still a foot deep on the lower ground. Water flows in narrow channels through ice six inches thick.

There are no blackbirds or thrushes in the valley now; no robins, hedge sparrows, or wrens. Only two feeble skylarks are left of the hundreds that were here in autumn. Three chaffinches remain from a flock of three hundred. Jackdaw numbers have been halved. Fifty woodpigeons have survived the shooting and the snow, but they are very thin and weak. Crows follow them everywhere, waiting for them to die. Two pairs of bullfinches have come through. There are blue tits and marsh tits in the woods, and a flock of long-tailed tits. There are eighty mallard and forty red-legged partridges in fields by the brook.

I found the remains of thirteen woodpigeons and a mallard; all had been killed recently by the peregrine, and had been plucked and eaten on the surface of the snow. The mallard was lying in the open field a hundred yards from South Wood. After striking down its prey, the peregrine had landed four yards away. There were two deep footprints in the

snow, at the end of long, scored grooves. On each side were
lighter scuffing marks made by the tips of the hawk's wings.
Shallower footprints led up to the kill and were clustered
around it. Light parallel lines showed where the end of the
hawk's tail had dragged along the snow. The prints of the
three front toes were short and blunt; that of the hind toe
was three inches long, and was more deeply embedded. The
tracks of a fox came out to the kill, and went back into the
wood again. It had smelt the blood of the duck, and had
gnawed the bones when the hawk had finished feeding.

February 22nd. The slow thaw continues, and birds are returning to the valley. Today there were three hundred fieldfares in trees by the brook. Blackbirds and chaffinches were in
the woods, and a skylark sang. A hundred mallard, twenty
woodpigeons, and a mute swan, were feeding on a heap of
potatoes. They flew off together when I approached, and
manœuvred together as a flock before returning to their food.
There were many fox and hare tracks in the snow, broken by
flattened hollows where the animals had rolled about in it,
presumably for pleasure, as dogs do.

I found more peregrine kills: six woodpigeons and a rook.
One of the woodpigeons had been killed only an hour or
two before; its blood was still being absorbed by the snow.
The wings, breast-bone, legs, and pelvis, lay at the centre of a
widely scattered circle of blowing feathers. The deep corru-
gated toe marks of the peregrine were mixed with the spidery
footprints of a crow and the pad marks of a fox. Both fox
and crow had apparently tried to drive the hawk from its
kill. A large area of snow had been trampled by their feet.
The scaly rings and bumpy pads of the hawk's toes, which
help it to grip its prey, had made deep dents in the snow.
These odd, thick-toed, knobbly footprints are quite different
from those of other birds. To rest my hand in the place where

the peregrine had stood so recently was to experience a strong feeling of proximity, of identification. Footprints in snow are strangely moving. They seem an almost shameful betrayal of the creatures that make them, as though something of themselves had been left defenceless. The valley is covered with the footprints of birds that the cold weather has killed, pathetic memorials that the sun is slowly eroding.

At midday the tiercel circled in hazy sunshine and drifted away in the south-east wind. I tried to follow, but the snow was too deep for me. Ditches and gullies have been filled in and hidden. One can plunge without warning into six feet of snow.

All through the clear afternoon, little owls called, magpies flashed in the sun, and migrating gulls circled north-east. They flew high, and I could not see them without binoculars. Their loud cackling cries came down from an empty sky.

February 27th. The days are cloudless now. The cold east wind is a blaze of lances, the sun warm and brilliant in wide skies. The snow steadily recedes, and the parched eye is quenched with green again. Strange unfamiliar green, like green snow fallen on white fields.

Two hundred woodpigeons have come back, jays are conspicuous again, fieldfares thrive. Hedge sparrows feed in the lanes, and there are blackbirds everywhere. A song thrush and four skylarks sang all day. I flushed seven pairs of red-legged partridges and numerous coveys.

There were thirty kills in the fields by the brook, and between the two woods: twenty-six woodpigeons, a moorhen, and three fieldfares. Almost all were old, and had been covered by snow until now. One very fresh woodpigeon had been plucked and eaten on the brook's only remaining stretch of ice. For the last two months woodpigeons have been thin and under-weight, and the peregrines have had to kill a larger number than usual to obtain the amount of food they need.

At three o'clock the tiercel circled among rooks to the east of the ford. Later, between branches, I saw his bronze-brown back gleaming in yellow sunlight as he perched on an oak. He shone like a huge, inverted, golden pear.

March 2nd. This was the eighth successive cloudless day, and the burnished blue of the sky shone as though it could never again be hidden. The strong south-east wind was cold, but the sun's warmth made the snow seem utterly vanquished and senile, sent it slithering waterily down into the rising land.

Woodpigeons and jackdaws went up from North Wood at midday, and cawing crows flew to their tree-top stations. Chaffinches by the bridge scolded steadily for ten minutes, their monotonous 'pink, pink' gradually dying away in the sunlit silence. I saw nothing. Assuming the hawk to have soared down wind, I searched for him north of the ford and found him in the dead oak half an hour later. He flew up into the wind and began to circle. His wingbeats became shallower, till only the tips of his wings were faintly fluttering. I thought he would soar, but instead he flew quickly south-east. The lane that divides North Wood dips and rises through a steep-sided gulley, which is sheltered from the wind. The peregrine has learnt that warm air rises from the sunny, windless slopes of the lane, and he often flies there when he wishes to soar.

Slowly he drifted above the orchard skyline and circled down wind, curving upward and round in long steep glides. He passed from the cold white sky of the south, up to the warm blue zenith, ascending the wind-bent thermal with wonderful ease and skill. His long-winged, blunt-headed shape contracted, dwindled, and darkened to the flinty point of a diamond as he circled high and far over; hanging and drifting above; indolent, watchful, supreme. Looking down, the hawk saw the big orchard beneath him shrink into dark twiggy lines and green strips; saw the dark woods closing together and reaching out across the hills; saw the green and white fields turning to brown; saw the silver line of the brook, and the coiled river slowly uncoiling; saw the whole valley flattening and widening; saw the horizon staining with distant towns; saw the estuary lifting up its blue and silver mouth, tongued with green islands. And beyond, beyond all, he saw the straight-ruled shine of the sea floating like a rim of mercury on the surface of the brown and white land. The sea, rising as he rose, lifted its blazing storm of light, and thundered freedom to the land-locked hawk.

Idly, indifferently, he saw it all, as he swung and swayed round the glittering gun-sight of his eye's deep fovea, and watched for a flash or spurt of wings at which to aim his headlong flight. I watched him with longing, as though he were reflecting down to me his brilliant unregarded vision of the land beyond the hill.

He passed across the sun, and I looked away to wring the hot purple from my eyes. When I found him again, he was high to the west of the sun, hidden in the excoriating blueness of the sky till the binoculars drew him down. Head to wind, like a compass needle cleaving to the north, he drifted, steadied, and hung still. His wings closed and curved back, then opened and reached forward, splaying out wide like an owl's. His tail tapered like a dart, then opened in a broad spreading fan. I could see the gaps in his wings, where the feathers he shed in December had not yet been replaced. When he banked in the sun, he flashed from blackness to fire and shone like white steel. Poised on two thousand feet of sunlit air, he commanded the birds of the valley, and none flew beneath him. He sank forward into the wind, and passed slowly down across the sun. I had to let him go. When I looked back, through green and violet nebulæ of whirling light, I could just see a tiny speck of dusk falling to earth from the sun, flashing and turning and falling through an immense silence that crashed open in a tumult of shrilling, wing-beating birds.

I became aware of my own weight, as though I had been floating upon water and was now beached and dry and clothed and inglorious again. The hawk had soared for twenty minutes; during all that time blackbirds had been scolding in the hedge behind me and partridges had called in the fields. The stoop silenced them like death. And then the only sounds were the whisper and rustle of melting snow—a faint fluttering like a mouse in dry grass—and the tinkle and chime of a small stony stream, bearing it down to the brook.

The hawk had gone, and I walked in the fields in a haze of contentment, waiting for him to come back. He usually returns to his favourite perching places at intervals during the day. Although I had lost touch with him from the end of December till now, it was obvious that he remembered me and was still comparatively approachable and tame. Song thrushes, blue tits, and great tits, sang; a great spotted woodpecker drummed. Throughout the afternoon, hundreds of migrating gulls circled high to the north-east, drifting and calling.

At three o'clock I had a pricking sensation at the back of the neck that meant I was being looked at from behind. It is a feeling that must have been very intense to primitive man. Without turning round, I glanced over my shoulder to the left. Two hundred yards away, the hawk was perched on the low horizontal branch of an oak. He was facing north and glancing back at me over his left shoulder. For more than a minute we both stayed still, each puzzled and intrigued by the other, sharing the curious bond that comes with identity of position. When I moved towards him, he flew at once, going quickly down through the north orchard. He was hunting, and the hunter trusts no one.

Half an hour later he came skimming over the orchard from the east, and landed abruptly in an apple tree. He never slows down before landing; a foot from his intended perch he simply spreads his wings to stall, stops, and drops lightly down. I was standing at the south-west corner of the orchard, with my back to the sun, and the hawk ignored me. His long yellow toes shifted and flexed and bulged as they gripped the central stump of the tree, his head jerked and twisted about, the feathers of his crown bristled up into a crest. The dark feathers of the moustachial bars stood out in relief against the white cheek patches. He was hunting. Rage shone from his glaring eye. I knew it; all the orchard birds were talking of it. Partridges called, blackbirds scolded; distant magpies, jays, and crows, cursed and muttered and kept low.

The hawk flew down towards the brook and rose beyond it, turning and slanting up across the wind, tilting and swaying up in steep spirals. His loose wings beat quickly, as though he were shaking them inside out. The sun was low now, and the air very cold. I did not think it was warm enough for a hawk to soar in, but at three hundred feet he levelled out and glided away down wind in long easy circles. When I could only just see him, and he was very high and far beyond the river—over a mile away—all the birds in the orchard around me were in a greater panic than before, crouching low and calling endlessly, shrilling in wild alarm. If a hawk is high in the sky, no matter how far distant, no bird feels safe; but a hawk hidden is a hawk gone and forgotten.

After much circling and hovering he saw prey to the south-east, and slid slowly away towards it in a long descending glide. Two hours to sunset; the western sky a golden mist of light, the wide ploughlands hazed in grey. The hawk cut down through the strong wind, beating his wings and gliding, his speed steadily increasing. Then he swept forward into a fast shallow glide, with his wings curving back and bending inwards, till he was moulded to the rigid spearhead shape of the stoop. A flock of starlings rose in front of him, and flew south as fast as they could. The hawk rushed over and beyond them in a second. They seemed to flick back beneath him as though they had never moved. He flowed across the dazzling sky in one great slash of light, and flared out into the darkness of the trees. I did not see him again, but long after he had gone the bird-clouds rose and fell above the southern skyline, like the calm drift of smoke above the rage and fire of battle.

March 5th. The snow is neolithic, eroded by the warm south wind. Snow tumuli crumble where the great drifts rose against the sky. The whole valley ripples with running water. Ditches are streams, streams brooks, the brook a river, the river a chain of moving lakes. Lapwings and golden plover have come back. All day the lapwing flocks were passing over to the north-west. I looked at them in binoculars and found larger flocks above them, flying much higher, invisible to the unaided eye.

By half past three I had given up searching for the peregrine and was sitting glumly on a gate near the dead oak. When he suddenly flew past me, I was lifted to joy on the surge of his wings. There was a zestful buoyancy, a lilting eagerness in his rushing-past, boring, dipping, swaying, curving-up flight. He perched in a tree to the east and looked back at me. I felt that I had been found. He crouched on a low branch in the crabbed, uneasy, sidling stance that means he is hunting. Among the many gnarled branches of the oak he was hard to pick out. After five minutes desperate rest he flew off to the eastern orchard. Rising and falling, he went switchbacking over the wind, and dashed down at fieldfares that rose from the trees. I followed him through the long orchard aisles. Blackbirds were still scolding, and hundreds of fieldfares were skirmishing, but the hawk had gone. I went back to the gate.

At half past four the jackdaw cloud above the brook lifted and scattered as the peregrine came through. Sweeping down wind, he sailed splendidly up from the south, wings held high in a 'V,' swaying and gliding at speed. He was all wind-borne and flowing. He swept on towards north orchard, skimmed over the boundary poplars, curved down in a tremendous wing-lit parabola. I did not see him again.

During the day's long tramp I found forty-nine kills: forty-five woodpigeons, two pheasants, a red-legged partridge, and a blackbird. Only the last two were recent; the rest had been hidden under snow for a long time.

March 6th. Still the warm south wind renewing, the sun warm, the air light and clear. Yellowhammers sang in the lanes, and there were chaffinch flocks in the orchards. Black-headed gulls came into the valley from the south, and soared above the river. They turned where the river turns, spiralled high above the ridge, and floated away north-east. They circled higher than the lapwing flocks, which were again moving in from the coast. Some lapwings flew down to join the large numbers that have gathered now in the valley fields, but most went steadily north-west.

By two o'clock I had been to all the peregrine's usual perching places, but had not found him. Standing in the fields near the north orchard, I shut my eyes and tried to crystallise my will into the light-drenched prism of the hawk's mind. Warm and firm-footed in long grass smelling of the sun, I sank into the skin and blood and bones of the hawk. The ground became a branch to my feet, the sun on my eyelids was heavy and warm. Like the hawk, I heard and hated the sound of man, that faceless horror of the stony places. I stifled in the same filthy sack of fear. I shared the same hunter's longing for the wild home none can know, alone with the sight and smell of the quarry, under the indifferent sky. I felt the pull of the north, the mystery and fascination of the migrating gulls. I shared the same strange yearning to be gone. I sank down and slept into the feather-light sleep of the hawk. Then I woke him with my waking.

He flew eagerly up from the orchard and circled above me, looking down, his shining eyes fearless and bland. He came lower, turning his head from side to side, bewildered, curious. He was like a wild hawk fluttering miserably above the cage of a tame one. Suddenly he jerked in the air as though shot, stalled, wrenched himself violently away from me. He defecated in anguish of fear, and was gone before the white necklace of sun-glittered fæces reached the ground.

March 7th. A day of endless wind and rain, which I wasted away in the lee of hollow trees, in sheds and barns, and under broken carts. I saw the hawk once, or thought I saw it, like a distant arrow flicking into a tree, blurred and distorted by the million shining prisms of the rain.

All day the unquenchable skylarks sang. Bullfinches lisped and piped through the orchards. Sometimes a little owl called lugubriously from its hollow tree. And that was all.

March 8th. I went out at four o'clock. The evening of the night was dark, and the warm west wind blew wet. Owls were calling in the long dim twilight before dawn. At six o'clock the first lark sang, and soon there were hundreds of larks singing up into the brightening air. Straight up from their nests they rose, as the last stars rose up into the paling sky. Rooks cawed as the light increased, and gulls began to fly inland. Robins, wrens, and thrushes, sang.

In the flat fens near the coast I lost my way. Rain drifted

softly through the watery green haze of fields. Everywhere there was the sound and smell of water, the feeling of a land withdrawn, remote, deep sunk in silence. To be lost in such a place, however briefly, was a true release from the shackles of the known roads and the blinding walls of towns.

By seven o'clock the sky was clear again. I climbed on to the coast wall just as the sun was rising. Quickly it pierced the rim of the sea; a huge, red, hostile, floating sun. As it lifted heavily off into the sky, light flashed and shattered from it, and it was a globe no longer.

A hen-harrier rose from its roosting place on the saltings and flew to the wall. It hovered low above the withered grass, which moved dryly in the draught from its wings. It was coloured like the waving grass: grey-brown and fawn and reddish-brown. The ends of its wings were black, and its long brown tail was barred and mottled light and dark. At the base of its tail the brilliant white splash of its upper tail coverts shone in the sunlight. It flew slowly into the wind, keeping low, beating its wings twice and then reaching them above its back in a 'V' as it glided forward with the dark primaries splaying open and curling upward. It hovered again, and glided down over the steep sides of the wall in long banking curves. It crossed from side to side, drifting over the grass still glittering with rain, lightly, softly, silently riding over the bending grass and looking down through the parting stems for prey. Imperceptibly it drifted away and was lost as suddenly as a shadow is lost when the sun goes in.

Slowly the wind dropped, and the air became warmer. The sun shone through a thin parchment of high cloud. Distance lengthened. Horizons sharpened as the morning grew. The grey sea dwindled out, mumbling with a line of foam the far edges of the shining mud beyond the vast moorland of the saltings. The remote farms and villages clustered up along the top of the empty inland fields. Redshanks chased and fretted over the broad dyke that runs beside the wall. More rain was coming, but for the moment all was still.

At half past ten, clouds of small birds sprayed up from the fields and a merlin cleaved through them like an arrow, dipping and darting. It was a thin narrow falcon, flying low. It swept over the sea-wall, curved out across the saltings, and swung up into steep spirals, its long sting-like body swaying in the blur of its jabbing, flicking wings. It flew fast, yet its wide circling seemed laborious and its rising slow. At three hundred feet it came round in a long curve, and poised, half-hovering. Then it flew forward into the wind towards a skylark singing high above the fields. It had seen the lark go up, and had circled to gain height before making an attack. From behind, the merlin's wings looked very straight. They seemed to move up and down with a shallow flicking action, a febrile pulsation, much faster than any other falcon's. It reached the lark in a few seconds, and they fell away towards the west, jerking and twisting together, the lark still singing. It looked like a swallow chasing a bee. They rushed down the sky in zigzags and I lost them in the green of the distant fields.

Their rapid, shifting, dancing motion had been so deft and graceful that it was difficult to believe that hunger was the cause of it and death the end. The killing that follows the hunting flight of hawks comes with a shocking force, as though the hawk had suddenly gone mad and had killed the thing it loved. The striving of birds to kill, or to save themselves from death, is beautiful to see. The greater the beauty the more terrible the death.

March 9th. The morning sun was low and dazzling, and the wind cold, as I walked along the sea-wall by the north shore of the estuary. A falcon peregrine startled me by her sudden upward leap from the lee of the wall, where she had been hidden. I was directly above her, looking down at the long tapering span of her wings and the humped width of her back. She rose quite silently, like a short-eared owl, and flitted away across the marsh, rocking violently from side to side, tilting between two vertical planes, standing in air on the tip of each wing in turn. When a long way off, she glided slowly down into the grass. I could not find her again. She had been sleeping in the sun—perhaps after bathing—and had not heard me coming.

Heavy rain fell in the afternoon. The falcon flew up to a dead oak, near the sea-wall, and watched the waders gathering on the saltings at high tide. She was still there when I left, huddled and sombre in the pouring rain, as whistling wigeon drifted in with the tide and the babble of waders grew louder.

March 10th. Towering white clouds grew in the marble sunlight of the morning. The wind eroded them to falling weirs of rain. The estuary at high tide brimmed with blue and silver light, then tarnished and thinned to grey.

A falcon flew low across the marsh, weaving through the wind with sudden dips and swerves, as though moving under invisible branches and twisting between invisible trees. She flew like a big, sleepy merlin. The sun shone on the splendid burnish of her back and wings. They were a deep roan colour, the colour of a redpoll steer, like the patches of red soil that stain the ploughlands to the north. The primaries were black, with a tint of blue. The comma-shaped curl of the dark brown moustachial mark gleamed like a nostril on the white face. The hump of muscle between her wings rose and fell under the feathers as the wings moved forward and back. She looked docile, yet menacing, like a bison. Redshanks stood sleekly in the grass and watched her go by. They were quite still, save for the nervous bobbing and twitching of their bright orange legs.

An hour later, from a flurry and cry of curlew, the falcon lifted clear and circled slowly up above the marsh. She glided in a thermal of warm air that bent its white bloom of cloud before the strong north wind. With rigid wings outstretched, she rose in a trance of flight, wafted upon air like a departing god. Watching the falcon receding up into the silence of the sky, I shared the exaltation and serenity of her slow ascension. As she dwindled higher, her circles were widened and stretched out by the wind, till she was only a sharp speck cutting across white cloud, a faint blur on blue sky.

She drifted idly; remote, inimical. She balanced in the wind, two thousand feet above, while the white cloud passed beyond her and went across the estuary to the south. Slowly her wings curved back. She slipped smoothly through the wind, as though she were moving forward on a wire. This mastery of the roaring wind, this majesty and noble power of flight, made me shout aloud and dance up and down with excitement. Now, I thought, I have seen the best of the peregrine; there will be no need to pursue it farther; I shall never want to search for it again. I was wrong of course. One can never have enough.

Far to the north the falcon tilted downward and slid slowly through sun and shadow towards earth. As her wings swept up and back, she glided faster. And then faster, with her whole body flattened and compressed. Bending over in a splendid arc, she plunged to earth. My head came forward with a jerk as my eyes followed the final vertical smash of her falling. I saw fields flash up behind her; then she was gone beyond elms and hedges and farm buildings. And I was left with nothing but the wind blowing, the sun hidden, my neck and wrists cold and stiff, my eyes raw, and the glory gone.

March 11th. I spent the day on the south side of the estuary, walking in the wet fields and searching for hawks in the long tree-hedges and the warm, lark-hung sky. I found none, but it was a happy day.

West of the flat estuary plain there are small dome-shaped hills with deep valleys between them. At six o'clock the light above these hills was brightening towards sunset. The valley fields were shaded and sombre. Flickering through the dark shadows of the trees, below the lane where I was standing, the tiercel peregrine circled up towards the light. He flew fast, banking in narrow turns, winding in steep spirals, wings lashing and quivering. Soon he was high above me. He could see the hills sinking down into the shadowed valleys and the far woods rising all around, the towns and villages still in sunlight, the broad estuary flowing into blue, the grey dimness of the sea. All that was hidden from me was shining clear to his encircling eye.

From the coiled spring of his spirals he suddenly shot forward, cleaving to the north with savage power, dipping, twisting, swerving, his long wings leaping and bouncing from the air. He was desperate with the rage of the hungry hawk.

Light fades, and prey moves closer to the lurking dusk, and the last lark rises, and the night—so long forgotten—suddenly throws black shadows across the blazing brilliance of the eye.

Searing through the sky, the hawk in torment saw the land beneath him work and seethe with birds and come alive. Golden plover broke their wild cries along the green surface of the lower air. The peregrine hissed among them like a burning brand.

March 12th. The valley is flooded now, and the tiercel is hunting and bathing in the higher, greener lands to the south and east. Between the valley and the long, narrow estuary I found him soaring in the strong north wind. He soared, and hovered, and flew south. Sped by the following wind, I cycled frantically along the winding lanes, keeping that high, forked speck in view, losing it, then coming up with it again as it paused to soar above feeding flocks of gulls and plover. Rooks perched by their bulky nests in tall hill-cresting elms, cawing warm-throatedly to the strong March sun. Trees smudged black as charcoal against the clear green light.

I swung over the hills and down into the deep valley, seeing the tiercel diving down the fanned sun's rays towards the distant marshes. I swooped through leicestershires of swift green light. A dazzling wetness of green fields irrigated the windswept eye. The humming wheels plunged away below me; I was dragged down in a rush of wind. This was hunting speed, pounding after the winged hawk quick to the quarry. I remembered galloping over springy green turf, as a child; over the neglected, fallen farm-land of pre-war years; through the wild hedges and the glorious wastes of flowering weeds flaming with hawks and finches.

The far hills turned, revolved, shifted apart; the lean silver length of the long estuary suddenly shone out to the horizon like a spar of light, and all the distant marshes floated up to the thin blue surface of the sea. I stopped, and stood above the green flush of the marshland. The peregrine hurled towards the gap of light that was the sea, ricocheting across the green land like a swift rebounding flame.

March 13th. A mistle thrush sang by the ford, the first of the year, rolling out his rich mellow phrases. He stopped singing, and dashed into the copse. I heard the dry rattle of his scolding note; then he chased a peregrine across to the dead oak.

It was a tiercel, one I had not seen before, shorter-winged and more compactly built than the bird that has wintered in the valley, darker and browner in colour with no red or gold in his plumage. There were gaps in his wings and tail where moulted feathers had not yet been replaced. For a long time he did nothing, though he often looked up at the sky, tilting his head far back to watch the high drifting specks of the migrating gulls.

After an hour of idleness he glided gently away from the tree, down to the green corn in the field in front of him. He rose up almost at once, with a thick red earthworm dangling from his toes. Dodging the rushes of a screeching gull, he bent his head down to meet his uplifted foot and ate the worm in three gulping bites. He returned to the oak, and the gull flew off. Gulls have been flying over these fields for a week or more, dropping down at intervals for worms. Curiosity may have induced the watching hawk to do the same. Three times, during the late afternoon, he planed down to the field to catch and eat a worm. It had begun to rain, and many worms were coming to the surface.

Between these flights, the hawk slept with his head sunk down into his breast feathers, featureless as an owl. The heavy rain did not disturb him, and he was soon bedraggled and sodden. In the early dusk he flew to a higher perch, in an elm at the edge of north orchard. I was able to stand under the tree and look up at him through the drab rainy light. Though he was very sleepy, he woke at the slightest sound or movement and glared intently down at the calls of the partridge coveys. His feathers hung thickly, like wet fur. He looked like a Red Indian stalker with all but his head concealed in shaggy buffalo hide.

March 14th. Along the southern shore of the estuary the water dwindled out in shallows of shining silver-blue. Widening strands of mud gleamed yellow in the sun. Three curlew landed on the mud, and stepped delicately to the water's edge. They were uneasy, moving their heads from side to side like deer suspicious of the wind. They were coloured like sand, and mud, and shingle, and the sere grass of the saltings. Their legs were the colour of the sea.

A peregrine flew over, and hovered above the sea-wall where partridges were crouching in the grass. It was a lion-coloured tiercel, fierce and proud, looking down with luminous, dark, liquescent eyes. Where the wide wings joined the chest the feathers underneath were thickly mottled with diamond-shaped spots, like the fur of a snow leopard. The amber hawk glowed briefly in the sun, then flew inland.

I went up the long slope of fields to the east of the creek, and found a falcon peregrine resting in an oak at the top. Her feathers were wet. She was drying them after bathing in a flooded field. Her big chest was a blend of brown and tawny arrowheads, but the lower feathers were darker and less yellow, hanging thick and loose over the branch of the tree. Her gnarled feet shone like polished brass. Her head was never still. From her high perch she could see all movement in the fields and creeks and along the miles of ochre shore.

I was very close before she bothered to look at me with both eyes at once. I walked nearer. Without hesitation or fuss, she spread her wings and let the light breeze lift her from the tree. The long tapering primaries were stretched out, and the broad fan-like secondaries spread wide, their pale barred surfaces shimmering with air. Gliding and gently feathering forward, the large hawk rippled from the tree and rowed out on to the blue water-air above the creek. Turned and floated by the breeze, she drifted down the soft swath of the estuary sky to the bright sea-sky beyond.

Heavy clouds lowered, and the afternoon was dull. Mustard yellow in the dusky light, a short-eared owl rose silently from a ditch, floated up like a buoyant moon, with no sound but the soft rustle of the parting grass. Turning its cat-like face towards me, it flexed its mottled snakeskin wings across the marsh.

High tide brimmed grey and glossy in the creek. The short-eared owl beat slowly out above its own reflection, looking like two owls striving to meet through the water's shining skin. One rose above the sea-wall as the other dived below.

March 15th. A brilliant south-west gale, broken sunlight, warm white clouds. Plover circled in the gusty air, golden nebulæ receding down the blue reaches of the northern sky. The sky's horizon lies far beyond the earth's. High birds shine in that bright corona long after lower ones have dulled into the iron rim beneath. Lapwings rose to the soaring hawk—hooked bill, barbed talons hidden—like fish rising to a gay resplendent fly. They are lured to the sky and are killed as they rise. Once high they are safe, but they die as they rise.

At half past twelve the dark brown tiercel perched on the straggling east-west hazel hedge that bisects north orchard. He was sunning himself after bathing, while the golden tiercel hunted the valley. Occasionally he flew up into the gale, hovered, then planed down to the hedge again. At two o'clock he flew with more determined wing-beats, flicking forward with quick, short jabs. He hovered for a moment, swooped with wings half closed, and plunged into the sere grass between the apple trees, feet lowering and wings spreading wide. He rose huddled, and flapped heavily down to the brook, carrying a red-legged partridge and a long red stalk of seeding dock. The partridge had reached up to eat the seeds of the dock. The hawk had seen the movement and had pounced on the partridge before it had finished feeding, had lifted stalk and bird together from the ground.

He returned an hour later, and perched in an apple tree at the edge of open ploughland. I sat and watched him from thirty yards, away from all cover. After two minutes of uneasy glaring, he flew straight at me as though intending to attack. He swept up into the wind before he reached me, and hovered twenty feet above my head, looking down. I felt as a mouse must feel, crouching unconcealed in shallow grass, cringing and hoping. The hawk's keen-bladed face seemed horribly close. The glazed inhuman eyes—so foreign and remote—swivelled like brown globes in the long sockets of the moustachial bars. The badger-coloured face was vivid and sharp against the sky. I could not look away from the crushing light of those eyes, from the impaling horn of that curved bill. Many birds are snared in the tightening loop of his gaze. They turn their heads towards him as they die. He returned to the tree, unsatisfied, and I left him alone for a while.

From two o'clock till five he rested on the hazel hedge or hovered above the orchard. He was never out of my sight. He always perched on the highest twigs, however slender and pliant. Up and down, side to side, hawk and twig bent and swayed together in the gale. He kept his eye-level stable by grotesque dipping and twisting movements of his head and neck, as though he were constantly peering over the top or round the sides of an irritating obstruction. His big citron-yellow feet grasped the thin twig clumsily, one placed above the other, their polished scaly rings glinting in the sunlight. When he faced me, full-cropped and sleepy, he was so broad and barrel-chested that his wings did not show at all. Below his creamy throat, which was lightly flecked with brown, the feathers of his breast were ochreous or tawny, seamed vertically with chocolate brown and glowing in the sun like tarnished bronze. The dark brown moustache lobes hung down from lighter-coloured lateral bars above the eyes. The crown streaked vertically into a close wood-graining of red-dish-brown and buff, tinged with grey, and paler at the nape. The bulbous eyes were brown as malty woodland mud, deep sunk in sockets of pale turquoise skin. The cere was yellow; the base of the bill grey, the hooked tip blue.

He seldom looked at me, and he did not follow the movements of my hands. He was watching the long grass, and listening. Listening like an owl, with his facial feathers bristling, and his ear coverts lifting and falling. If he had eaten much of the partridge he could not have been hungry, yet he was obviously alert and unable to stop hunting. Sometimes he looked up at the gulls that were soaring north-east. They recognised him, and screamed harshly as they drifted away. Occasionally he turned his head right round so that he was facing the northern half of the orchard. Again, suddenly, he flew towards me and hovered overhead, looking curiously, indifferently down, as we look down at fish, so far removed from us by the reflecting curve of water that we can never fear them, unless we fall. The undersides of his wings were creamy yellow, overlaid by a narrow mesh of thin brown lines and a faint silvery sheen. The axillaries, and the inner halves of the secondary coverts, were spotted with darker brown or with larger, diamond-shaped marks.

Unable to soar because of the gale, he hovered persistently with wonderful power and control. He exhausted his hunting urge by hovering over every part of the orchard, but he did not go beyond its boundaries. At half past three, while he was perching, hundreds of plover circled high above the valley. The other tiercel was hunting again. By four o'clock the orchard tiercel was quieter. He stopped hovering, and flew slowly down to an elm. After preening, he opened his bill wide and puffed out his throat, like a pigeon cooing. This gaping, frog-like bulging in and out of his throat went on for ten minutes, while he scratched his throat feathers vigorously with one foot and wriggled his neck. Then he cast up his pellet of undigested bone and feather and went to sleep at once. Half an hour later he flew across the field to the dead oak, and slept there, completely at rest.

The wind had fallen, and clouds were larger and darker.

The golden-coloured tiercel swung low across the fields like a beam of light, and swept up to the highest branch of an elm, in a torrent of wing-beats. The long, rowing strokes of his wings were quite different from the shorter, jabbing beats of the brown tiercel. It was like comparing a borzoi with a collie. He perched for a moment, like a reddish-gold arrow suddenly wedged in a tree, then went plunging and leaping away to the north. The brown tiercel slept in the oak; he did not see the other hawk come or go.

After five o'clock the wind dropped completely. The evening was very calm. Released from the gale, the whole valley seemed to drift slowly southward.

March 16th. It was six o'clock, an hour before sunrise, when I stopped to watch a barn owl. It wavered up to the road, whitening and hardening out of the grey half-light, drifted across, and went softly down towards the river. There was a heavy breath of silence in the dew-damp fields. A second owl rose from the grass verge, and passed close. Its round white face looked slowly back, the big lolling head turned in wonderment. The dark prune-like eyes shone through the sad fool's mask of feathers. Then the long white wings came up and gathered the bird away into the fir wood, where night remained.

On the estuary the day was cold and clear. I saw the tide rise and turn, and watched waders feeding and at rest, while duck slept, and the sun moved west above the elm-crowned islands.

An hour before sunset I lay on the stone slope of the sea-wall, facing the golden-red fire of the dilating sun. The tide dwindled on the mud. The cold air sharpened, and began to smell of the coming night. With a roar of wings, like a cliff collapsing into the sea, every bird on the shore rose, leaving it bright beneath a wing-clouded sky. Wigeon flew overhead, sweeping up from the marsh behind the wall. There was a loud smacking sound like a plank hitting mud, a splash of falling excrement, and a harsh whistling of wings. The steeply climbing wigeon fanned apart. One fell back on to the marsh, huddled and slack, its narrow head hanging golden-crested from the drooping, shaking neck. It looked unreal, as though it should have spilt sawdust, not dripped blood. It lay where it fell, crumpled and spoilt.

The peregrine did not return to its kill while I was near. I had not seen it at all. It killed in the air above me and still I could not see it, so fast and sudden was its stoop. (When I went there next morning, it had already eaten and gone. The headless wigeon lay sacrificially upon its back, the creamy-whiteness of its bones gleaming in the sun above the dark bloodstains and the soft feathers lifting and falling in the wind.)

At dusk I saw a barn owl again, hunting between road and river. For twenty minutes it quartered the meadow, moving across in long, straight lines. Six feet above the grass it flew, with fast even wing-beats. The steady pulse of its wings was curiously soothing. Dusk deepened. The owl grew bigger and whiter. The rising moon turned from deep orange to yellow as it drifted clear of the trees. The owl rested on a gate-post, and I could see the bland meditative mask of its face looking at me from the grey of the field. The curved hook of its beak protruded from the heart-shaped disc of the mask, like a single claw. The dark eyes were rimmed with wine. It flew overhead, and in the first coldness of the spring night, suddenly called. A hoarse bellowing shriek drew out to a sharp edge, and bristled away to silence. But not the silence that was there before.

March 17th. Long scrolls and columns of cloud poured away in the grey east wind and made the sky seem endless. Light strengthened with the wind, was brilliant in the cold gale of afternoon, faded to mist and dusk an hour before sunset.

I walked out to the point, where the soft river light of the estuary meets the bleaker brightness of the sea. A large falcon peregrine flew low across the water towards the line of empty cargo ships moored in mid-stream. She swooped up to perch on the masthead of one of them, stayed there for five minutes, then flew towards the southern shore.

By half past four the light was very gloomy, and a short-eared owl was hunting over the marshes. A barn owl flew beneath it, and the larger owl swooped viciously at the smaller. The barn owl dived into the grass and stayed there for ten minutes. After this encounter the two owls kept apart, one in each half of the marsh. As the light slowly congealed, the brown owl was hidden, but the white owl grew whiter. They hunted in exactly the same manner, probably for the same prey.

Woodpigeons went up in clouds from trees near the farm, half a mile to the west. A thousand birds rose, clenched together, exploded outwards in a vast seething diffusion. A peregrine was hunting there, but I was too far away to see it.

In the early dusk I crossed the marsh and went up the lane towards the village. I was stopped by a startlingly loud scream, a shrill 'chow-week,' from a solitary lapwing in a field to the west. As it called it flew low and fast. Behind it, flying just above the furrows, the lean, racing shape of a tiercel peregrine glinted golden. His wings cleaved high above his back as he drew up to the lapwing with long, savage, rowing strokes. The lapwing gained by making sudden twists and turns, but the peregrine closed up in a second, turning in wider arcs but at greater speed. As the lapwing flew towards the cover of some bushes, the peregrine rose above it, hovered black against the sky, swooped vertically down. It was an appalling blow. The lapwing was banged into the earth. The two birds fell together; one slack and soft in death, the other tense with rage and shock. This solitary lapwing had stayed too late from the flock, lost in the ritual of its display and song. Trailing the dead bird in his foot, the peregrine flew over the darkening field to the marsh, where the white owl was still hunting.

March 20th. The drizzle of the morning thinned to mist, the mist gave way to cloud, but the day stayed damp and dull. The north-east wind was cold.

The dark brown tiercel returned to the orchard at eleven o'clock, cast his pellet from an elm, and flew off again. I found several pellets in the grass below the tree. All contained the fur and bones of mice, and some woodpigeon feathers. The tiercel reappeared at half past twelve, and stayed in or near the orchard for the rest of the day. He now has two dark blue-black adult feathers in the centre of each wing, and two blue-and-white barred feathers in the centre of his tail.

For three and a half hours he was still-hunting from high perches, from lombardy poplars or from alders or oaks by the brook, looking intently down into the orchard grass. The height of his perch was important to him. He landed on the highest twig of a poplar, looked around, then flew to one a few inches taller. After further peering, and measuring with his eye, he eventually flew to the tallest of the line. His foot-work was beautifully precise and nimble. He never fumbled his grasp of even the thinnest, bending twig. Often I stood only twenty yards from his perch, and saw him looking over my head into the orchard behind me. He had no fear. If I clapped my hands or shouted he would sometimes glance down at me, but only for a second. Without binoculars I could see his eyes, and every detail of his plumage. With them I could see the smallest features, such as the stiff rictal bristles quivering round the base of his bill. The feathers of his back, mantle, and secondaries, were closely barred dark brown and buff, and were tinted reddish. The upper tail coverts were plain reddish brown, lighter in colour than tail or mantle; the primaries were black. The scapulars were distinctive: barred black and gold, with a luminous golden sheen, like satin, which showed up at a great distance in dull light.

After much staring and peering, with his head never still, the hawk occasionally flew forward and up into the wind, hovered for twenty to thirty seconds, then went back to his perch. He did not stoop or make any sort of attack. Distant partridges called whenever he flew up, but those close by were hidden in the long yellow grass, and I flushed them from places where the hawk had hovered. He was back on his perch by then and was not interested in pursuit. Sparrows shrilled at him from bushes, hopping about in agitation, turning their small, angry faces upward. He ignored them, just as he ignored my vacuous, upturned face. He concentrated fanatically on his curiously unsuccessful hunting, or pretence of hunting.

Between two and three o'clock he became increasingly alert and restive. At three he flew south-east and out of sight. His orchard hunting was obviously over. He flew into the dead oak, an hour later, where he stayed till dusk. He caught and ate six worms. Each time, he simply planed down to the cornfield, picked up a worm in his talons, and carried it back to a branch of the oak. Holding it down with one foot he ate it slowly in four or five bites. All his movements were leisured and deliberate. He had the look of a gourmet relishing some rare seasonal delicacy. More substantial prey had been eaten earlier. Worms, like mice, are merely savouries, which moulting peregrines seem unable to resist.

March 21st. A tawny owl, long dead, lay at the edge of South Wood. I lifted its broad wings, and powder down puffed out of them like dust. When I threw the light dry carcass aside, the long talons caught uncannily in my gloves, as though they still had life. The gristly, powerful legs, feathered to the toes, end in these curved hooks, sharp and hard as steel needles. They seem imperishable. They will outlive the crumbling bones and the blowing feathers, as the grass grows tall above them.

Under a blackthorn, beside the brook, I found a freshly killed woodpigeon. Blossom was drifting down into the drying blood. A footpath runs between the two woods, and is separated from them by small thorn-hedged fields and a scattering of oak and elm. There is a dead tree to the south of the path: twenty feet of ruined elm, branchless, jagged at the top like a broken tooth. On this mossy fang the lighter, golden-coloured tiercel was resting. He flew east when I approached, circled, then drifted down towards me in a series of steep glides and stalls. I stood near the dead tree and watched his descent. The big rounded head, suspended between the rigid wings, grew larger, and the staring eyes appeared, looking boldly through the dark visor of the eye mask. There was no widening of the eyes in fear, no convulsive leap aside; he just came steadily down and glided past me, twenty yards away. His eyes were fixed on my face, and his head turned as he went past, so that he could keep me in view. He was not afraid, nor was he disturbed when I lowered and raised my binoculars or shifted my position. He was either indifferent or mildly curious. I think he regards me now as part hawk, part man; worth flying over to look at from time to time, but never wholly to be trusted; a crippled hawk, perhaps, unable to fly or to kill cleanly, uncertain and sour of temper.

Soon the high white clouds were breaking up, and melting in the sun. I kept the hawk on the move, hoping he would soar. At half past one, tired of being chased, he glided slowly up, spread his wings along the warm surface of the air, and rose from sight. Circling and drifting, he floated off into the sky till my eyes saw only a sharp speck piercing through the blue, then nothing. Using binoculars, I found him again, cutting long graceful arcs across feathers of white cloud above the wooded ridge. I lay on my back on the dry earth, and watched him slowly shrink and fade. He created beautiful patterns and doodles in the sky, as swiftly evanescent as the swirling shapes of waves upon the shore. The sun was warm, hedges were fretted with green, larks sang up beneath the soaring hawk. There was firmness of heart in the land at last.

The hawk passed up into the lighter air above the hills, and I lay contentedly among the small sounds of the field, awaiting his return. Twenty minutes later he drifted back from the east and began slowly to descend. He swept to and fro across the wind, circling in figures of eight, crossing above the foot-path and circling over the fields on either side. When each figure was completed, he glided straight forward above the path, moving very smoothly and fast into the wind, with wings curved back. Then he turned slowly into the next figure. He was using the long straight footpath as a guiding line. He came down a thousand feet in this way, but even when almost overhead he was still merely a speck in the sky. Through binoculars he was just recognisable as a hawk. Easily, ma-jestically, he subdued and rode upon the wind, soothing it down under the soft hollows of his wings, mastering the sudden tempests and spanning the deep concavities of the turbulent air.

A sudden lunge, a steep glide down towards North Wood, and the line has broken. The hawk dives down like a fish that is suddenly free. A woodpigeon flies above the wood, looks up, veers wildly, but flies on. The dark speck of the hawk plunges, dilates to colour, recoils like a gun as the golden feet flash forward to strike. Grey feathers spurt outwards and float upon the air. The dead pigeon threshes down into the trees. The hawk has gone. The air seems empty and slack.

Late in the afternoon I find the kill, lying on its back in swampy green ground between high thin birches and hornbeams. The footprints of the hawk are trampled deep in the mud; the pigeon's feet are clean. It has been hollowed out to the bone, like an ivory boat.

March 22nd. Clouds high, wind cold, horizons picked clean by the wind. The orchard tiercel, at twelve o'clock, perched in his usual elm above scolding blackbirds and chaffinches. He flew up wind and hovered, fluttering in the strong grip of the wind, sky showing between all his wide-splayed wing and tail feathers. Tiring, he glided south, went low through the orchard and out across the fields. Hundreds of feeding jackdaws and woodpigeons went up wildly, rose high, scattered, left the place completely. Jackdaws spiralled away east, woodpigeons climbed out of sight to the west.

The tiercel returned to the orchard, and kept watch from tree-tops for an hour. When crows chased him from a poplar, he began to fly faster, with longer and more determined wingstrokes. From then on, he was much more active and alert. There is often a time in the peregrine's day when he is becoming hungry, but is still reluctant or unready to hunt. If he is then disturbed, by man or by mobbing birds, he acts as though released from doubt, and begins to hunt at once.

After dodging away from the crows, he flew back to the elm where I had seen him earlier. He perched higher than before, leaning forward, flicking his head from side to side, restlessly shifting the grip of his feet. When he dived, and flowed down from the tree with wings uprising, his eyes were focused on something he had seen in the orchard. He flew carefully, softly, up wind, and glided slowly out across open ground. He stopped, hovered twenty feet up, then dropped gently down on his prey. He rose heavily and flew low between trees, carrying a red-legged partridge, one of a pair that had wandered too far from cover. I ran after him. He dropped the partridge, but went back for it immediately. His recovery of the prey was amazingly fast. He flicked down and up again like an eye blinking. Then he went out of the orchard and across the brook, flying with quick deep wing-beats, sinking nearly to the ground, rising again, sagging and rebounding like a woodpecker. A red-legged partridge weighs a pound to a pound and a half. The tiercel carried it for at least a mile at a speed between thirty and forty miles an hour.

March 23rd. Today was a whole season away from yesterday, warmed by a strong west wind and mellow sunlight, hazing down to yellow scented dusk. Three hundred golden plover fed in meadows by the river, with lapwings, gulls, and fieldfares. They moved slowly through the grass, like grazing cattle. Then every bird rose, as though a net had been twitched beneath them and had flung them up together into air. Small birds took to trees, gulls and plover to the sky. Six snipe flew with the plover, and stayed with them in their high gyrations.

Through this flickering web of wings I saw a peregrine flash in the sun, and a plover tumbling down. It took me a long time to find it, and the hawk had gone by then. The plover had been struck from below. There was a wound in its side, as though it had been stabbed with a thin-bladed knife. Some flesh had already been eaten from the breast. One of its legs was withered and useless. It is astonishing how unerringly a peregrine can select a deformed or abnormal individual from a large flock of apparently identical birds. It may be that even the slightest physical weakness or difference in plumage can disastrously affect a bird's ability to escape. Perhaps a sick bird does not wish to live.

As I entered the orchard, the dark tiercel glowed up to an

alder beside the brook and watched me walk between the
apple trees. He flew to the hazel hedge, and I sat down twelve
yards away from him. We looked at each other for a while,
but the hawk lost interest and began to watch the grass.
When he flew stiffly past me, I knew by the sharp jerking of
his wings that he had sighted prey. He hovered, dived into the
grass, rose with a mouse in his foot. He carried it across to
the dead oak and ate it there, tilting his head far back to
watch the shining southern sky, where the golden tiercel was
soaring to the coast and gulls were circling. When the long
trail of bird-clouds had passed below the hill, he went back to
the brook.

I kept very close to him as he hovered over the orchard or
rested in alders, but he ignored me completely. He looked
intently at the grass near my feet, seeing or hearing some
movement of which I was quite unaware, although I was
only two yards from it and the hawk was thirty. His eyes
followed this movement. Suddenly his head jerked up and he
flew quickly across to hover above the grass ten yards away.
He turned on his side, closed his wings, and stooped. It was a
fall of six feet only, but the technique of the stoop is the same
for six feet as for six hundred. He hit the grass hard, but
without impact, soft and silent as an owl. He rose from it
lightly, carrying a large dead mouse, which he took to an
apple tree and swallowed in two bites, first the head, then the
rest. All this was done within twenty yards of me and I did
not even have to keep still.

He rested for ten minutes, then hovered over the northern
half of the orchard, between the pond and the hazel hedge,
where the grass is shorter. He quartered the ground
thoroughly, and seemed keener than ever. Eating the second
mouse had increased his hunger. For half an hour he hovered
in the gusty wind, without resting. He stooped only once, and
missed. The sunlit orchard was very quiet, laned with pale

amber light. The only sounds were the songs of thrushes and blackbirds, muted by distance, the occasional call of a moorhen, the creak and rustle of twigs in the wind. The only movement was the silent threshing of the hawk's long wings beating through the sunlit aisles. Silent to me; but to mice in the short grass, to partridges hidden and dumb in long grass under the trees, his wings would rasp through the air with the burning whine of a circular saw. Silence they dread; when the roaring stops above them, they wait for the crash. Just as we, in the war, learnt to dread the sudden silence of the flying bomb, knowing that death was falling, but not where, or on what.

In the mellow sunlight of the warm unclouded spring, the peregrine shone and blinked behind the branches of the apple trees like a setting sun. When I walked through the orchard, he followed me, hovering above, hoping I would flush something for him. Down by the brook, a stoat came running and jumping through the tussocky grass and the brambles, carrying a water vole in his jaws, holding it high so that it did not drag in the grass. The soft vole, fat and flabby in death, was twice the size of the thin-flanked stoat. It was like a tiger carrying a bullock. I left the hawk to his patient hunting, and the stoat to his meal.

For one tiercel peregrine there is the cloudless sky, the wide valley, the hills, the estuaries, the sea itself; twenty paradisal miles of hunting land, a million birds to choose from, ten thousand feet of warm and windy air to sail and soar upon. For the other tiercel, just as strong, with the same sharp bill and biting feet, there is only the quiet corner of an orchard, an acre of grass and apple trees, a few mice, a partridge per haps, worms, and then sleep. He seems to be hypnotised by this small symmetry of trees. He is like a gambler who cannot resist just one more throw in the hope that his luck will change.

I went along the brook and up to the dead elm to see if the golden tiercel had come back from the coast. He was not there, so I sat down to wait in a corner of the field. The shadow of a big oak was imprinted on the bare earth in front of me, and I could see the shapes of small birds flitting through the phantom crown of branches. I was almost asleep when a kingfisher flew overhead and went down to the brook. I had never seen one against the sky before; always I had seen them lit from below by reflecting river light. Flying high over dry earth, against the matt surface of a cloud, it seemed a feebler and much less splendid bird. Wild things are truly alive only in the place where they belong. Away from that place they may bloom like exotics, but the eye will seek beyond them for their lost home.

The tiercel glided down from the east at one o'clock and settled in a small oak on the far side of the field. I crept along in the shadow of a blackthorn hedge till I was only forty yards away from him, with the sun behind me. He faced the sun, and soon became drowsy and slack on his feet. He drew one leg up into his feathers, and slept, waking frequently to preen and look around. Hawks sleep lightly. They wake to the movement of a leaf in the breeze, to the swaying whisper of grass, to the lengthening and shutting-off of shadows. They are fugitives who have escaped from everything but fear.

The sun lowered, and the hawk shone in the amber light, every feather sleek and burnished or rippling in the breeze. He shone in the network of contorted branches like a splendid copper vessel splashed with gold. The big eyes protruded slightly from the angle where the vertical moustachial lobes met the dark horizontal eye bars. The bare blue-grey skin surrounding them gleamed white whenever the hawk turned his head. The oaks and elms, the sky and clouds above, were all reflected in those brilliant sepia eyes, as though they were painted in miniature on a glaze as smooth as the white of an egg. They were strangely indolent eyes. Sometimes they seemed to dusk over with a faint purple bloom like the mineral film coating the lenses of binoculars or the bloom on the dark skin of a plum.

Between half past three and four the hawk became more alert, flexing his tail, shifting his feet about, looking around and glancing up at the sky with quick turns of his head. He flew without warning, circled up above the field, sailed out into a long glide as though intending to soar. The glide changed to a downward swoop, and as I followed him down I saw a pair of kestrels rising into view, flying low above the brook. The peregrine struck at them, and they dived into a tree together. The male kestrel flew away to the south, calling shrilly; the female stayed in the tree. The peregrine flew north, carrying the mouse that one of the kestrels had dropped. These kestrels were attacked because the tiercel is now defending a territory and will not tolerate other raptors there. He might have killed one of them if he had not seen the falling mouse. He was unable to resist his instinctive urge to follow it down and catch it.

The peregrine returned to his perch, but he did not relax at all. His eyes had lost their languor. They had a pale brown glare, like wintry sunlight shining through the thickness of a wood. He circled up into the warm blue haze and soared away down wind. The air was heavy and sweet-smelling, borne in the wind like pollen.

I knew he would not come back today, and all the birds around me knew it too. Woodpigeons began to move about again. A flock of them flew across the fields between the two woods, keeping close to the ground, never rising more than a yard above it. They feared the stoop, for many have died while crossing from wood to wood. The kestrels flew to the dead elm, tremulously calling. In the nettles at the foot of the tree I found pellets dropped there by both kestrel and peregrine. The peregrine's contained many woodpigeon feathers, and several large gritty stones an eighth of an inch across, with sharp points and edges. It picks them up, as an aid to digestion, when it bathes in the brook.

For an hour longer I scanned the distant ridges, while all around me birds sang and fed in peace. Imprisoned by horizons, I envied the hawk his boundless prospect of the sky. Hawks live on the curve of the air. Their globed eyes have never seen the grey flatness of our human vision.

It was high tide at the estuary. As the land light faded, the sky above would grow bright with the shine of brimming water. The peregrine would fall upon the scattered tribes of sleeping waders. Their wings would rise into the sunset, like smoke above the sacrifice.

March 25th. White waves swept over molten blue water, searing the warm sea-wall. The tide was rising. The sun-glittered estuary was bright with falls of shining birds. Shelduck floated into creeks and bays, or rested big and white on green marshes. Redshank and skylark sang. Lapwings tumbled and danced. Ringed plover pondered the waves, or shoaled above them silvery, like fish flying. One sang his deep song along the thinning edge of shore, 'cook-a-doo, cook-a-doo, cook-a-doo,' wings tilting and rolling. Slow majestic pintail rode high upon the water, a patrician elegance of brown and white, aloof and narrow-necked. Tree-fringed islands softened the splinters of white sea-wall that pierced out to the long horizon. Distant almond blossom shone like coral.

Pairs of partridges whirred dryly from the wall. At first their parched calls were quite unsynchronised. Then the jerked down-beating wings began to force out a diminishing throaty sound that gradually expired as the birds glided over a hedge and dropped to cover. They were like wound clockwork toys slowly spluttering into silence.

When the spring tide cleared the saltings, waders took to the sky, shimmering and skimming in grey and silver discs, spilling and raining down, then whirling up like waves lifted from the water. I kept hearing a curious snoring sound, followed by bubbling, like someone breathing in and then gargling. Occasionally I saw a trail of bubbles in the water. Eventually the dark, whiskered muzzle of a seal appeared above the surface, and then the whole sleek streaming head. He looked at me, breathed in, and dived below. Slowly he splashed and idled round the bay and out to the estuary again. It is a good life, a seal's, here in these shallow waters. Like the lives of so many air and water creatures, it seems a better one than ours. We have no element. Nothing sustains us when we fall.

A dead porpoise was humped upon the shingle, heavy as a sack of cement. The smooth skin was blotched with pink and grey; the tongue black, and hard as stone. Its mouth hung open like the nail-studded sole gaping from an old boot. The teeth looked like the zip-fastener of a gruesome nightdress-case.

I found sixteen peregrine kills: three black-headed gulls, a redshank, and a wigeon, on the shingle; five lapwings, two wigeon, a rook, a jackdaw, and a shelduck, on the marsh. The shelduck lay at the end of a long trail of feathers torn out by the ripping impact of the stoop. A black-headed gull had been plucked and eaten on the smooth green lawn of a summer bungalow. It lay at the exact centre, reclining in a mass of white feathers, like a dead flower among spilt petals.

Late in the afternoon, a falcon peregrine flew down the estuary; lean, majestic, big as a curlew. Far above, there were flocks of grey plover glittering in high sunlight like the pilot fish that swim before a shark. The falcon glided, and began to soar. Drifting in the warm west wind, she circled up and disappeared into the blue mist of the distant sky. Nothing happened. The tide was ebbing, and waders crowded the growing line of shore. Gulls began to move out from the land. Half an hour later, I was looking through binoculars at a flock of starlings flying high overhead, when I saw beyond them a dark speck that did not move. It did not move, but it grew larger. It grew larger very quickly. It was the falcon falling in a tremendous stoop. Coming straight down at me, it had not the shape of a bird. It was like a falling head, a shark's head dropping from the sky. It made a faint sighing that quickly hardened to a shrill whining sound, like the wind harping through high wires. A great black-backed gull obscured the peregrine for a second as it passed over towards the shore. Its yellow bill, red-spotted, gleamed in the sun; its cold, pale eyes looked down. It had its usual heavily indifferent expression. There was a loud slamming bang. The gull buckled like hot metal. Its head jerked and flopped. The falcon had struck it in the neck.

After the long, almost gradual descent, this final flinging blow seemed dazzlingly fast. The falcon hooked and tore the gull's neck apart with her hind talons. She shivered away from the impact, like a splinter of wood flying from a cut log. Then she curved gently out and up above the water, recovering control. From a hundred feet up, the gull slid down quite slowly and emptied itself out upon the shingle. The falcon dropped beside it, and began to feed. The flesh was peeled away. The raw bones stood to the sky, like the ribs of a wrecked ship.

March 27th. Soft, reflective, mooing sounds came from a small oak in the hedge beside the sea-wall. It was a hollow tree, with a short stubby bole, and a crown of branches growing outwards from the hollow centre. When I stood beside it, I could just see the top of a little owl's head above the rim of the bole. He knew I was there, and after a minute he walked up a branch to have a look at me. We were about ten feet apart. He blinked; first with both eyes, then with the left one only. He bobbed deeply at the knees in a sort of quick curtsy, and stretched his neck up till it was thin and elongated. The tufty white stripes above his eyes moved and crinkled. Then he looked away, as though suddenly embarrassed.

He walked a bit farther up the branch, watching his feet as he did so, and turned to have another look at me. Slowly I raised my binoculars. The owl was startled, and ducked his head. But he was also curious, and for several minutes he stared straight into the lenses. His huge round eyes were bright, yet quite expressionless, as though they had been painted on to his head. The black pupil was the same width as the vivid yellow iris. He blinked a lot, and the grey nictitating membranes clicked sickeningly across his eyes for a second, like a doll's eyes closing. He did not seem able to focus me. I felt I was without meaning for him. I was like one of those trick photographs of a familiar object; if it cannot be recognised it is just nothing at all. His interest gradually slackened and he began to look away. He forgot me quite suddenly, and fluttered down into the tree. I was outside and he was inside, and he had nothing to say to me.

A little owl's legs are surprisingly thick and powerful for so small a bird. They look slightly hairy, like an animal's legs. The whole bird looks completely out of proportion when perching, like a two-legged head. One must try not to be anthropomorphic, yet it cannot be denied that little owls are very funny to watch. In flight, they are just owls, but at rest they seem to be natural clowns. They do not know it, of course. And that makes them much funnier, for they always appear indignant, outraged, brimming over with choler. There is nothing funny about their sharp claws and rending beak. They are killers. That is what they are for. But whenever I see one close, in a tree, I laugh aloud.

At dusk, before hunting begins, they are different again. Their spring song is a single woodwind note, rising, hollow, full of sweet pathos. It sounds like a distant curlew calling in a dream. The owls answer one another across the fields and valleys as dusk gathers in the trees. Then the spring night comes, smelling of cold grass.

Leaving the owl to his fretful sleep, I walked along the sea-wall towards the mouth of the estuary. Quiet sunlight gleamed the falling tide. Over a ploughed field something snake-like slithered and swam. It was a stoat following the scent of its prey, moving keenly and fast. It ran up and down furrows, bounded across ridges, doubled back, looped, twisted, worked farther out into the field, then came back towards the edge again. It crouched, ran, sprang, and crept, quivering with excitement, seeing the vivid colour of a smell. It was like a man trying to escape from a maze. It leapt on to the marsh, and I saw its red-brown back undulating away towards a grazing rabbit that was big with disease and helpless as a bog-ged cow. But the stoat did not kill it. It survives, protected by the horror of its own private death.

A pair of shoveler landed in the fleet, hitting the water with a whooshing splash after stalling for a long time. The rich bishop's purple of the drake's belly glowed in the sun. He floated deep in the water, hanging his heavy bill like the low jowl of a bloodhound, his dark head shining green and glossy.

On the shingle beach I found the remains of two wood-pigeons, which a peregrine had killed quite recently. The high spring tide, by a ghoulish freak, had draped the headless carcass of the great black-backed gull on a strand of barbed wire, close to the sea-wall. That was a remarkable kill, even for a falcon. A great black-backed gull weighs four to five pounds, a falcon two to two and a half. The flayed carcass of the gull was as heavy as a full-fleshed woodpigeon. These big gulls are messy, absent-minded killers. I was not sorry to see one die.

A flock of twenty bar-tailed godwits fed at the tide's edge with curlew and grey plover. One godwit was very restless. It flew over the mud-flats, plunging and cork-screwing wildly, tossing and slashing its long bill about like a fencer's foil. It careered erratically from one group of waders to another, swooping and flinging up above them, flushing dunlin, putting up duck from the saltings. It seemed to be deliberately mimicking the attack of a hawk. Its actions were remarkably like those of a hunting peregrine. If I had not been able to see the length of its bill, I would, at a distance, have mistaken it for a hawk. It is very curious that, an hour later, a tiercel peregrine came quickly from inland and swooped at waders in just the same way as the godwit had been swooping. He chased a godwit for several minutes, and eventually disappeared beyond the island, still in close pursuit.

At four o'clock, tiercel and falcon soared above the estuary together. A heron rose from feeding in the shallows, and flew heavily inland towards its nest. I expected to see the two peregrines stoop at it in the spectacular manner so often described in books about falconry. But they did not stoop. The falcon ignored the heron. The tiercel swooped past it and attacked it from below, chattering round its head like a monkey. When the heron disgorged a fish, the tiercel dived after it and made several attempts to catch it, but without success. Then he soared up to rejoin the falcon, and they circled out of sight across the marshes to the north.

Day ended with moonlight on the water. Brilliant stars appeared, many birds called, lights glimmered out across the estuary. Red clouds shone above the inland west.

March 28th. All day the south-west wind rose. The warm, sunlit air of morning towered away to clouds. At eleven o'clock, two hundred woodpigeons clattered up from the orchard as the dark brown tiercel arrived there from the south. I had just entered at the eastern end. We met by the brook. For an hour he watched and hovered, perching on many trees. He caught a mouse. To me he was still apparently indifferent, but he kept me in sight, when I moved, by following or flying higher. He has found a meaning for me, but I do not know what it is. I am his slow and moribund companion, Caliban to his Ariel.

Each time I have seen him he has tried to soar, but the weather has not been favourable. His attempts have been feeble and tentative. At half past twelve today he tried again. He rose to three hundred feet, turned, and glided down wind. He wanted to pull out of the glide into an upward circle, but he was travelling too fast. He flashed above the orchard, folded his wings back, and stooped to perch on the hazel hedge. After another half hour of restless flying and hovering, he returned to the hedge. I sat with my back against an apple tree, watching the hunched, unhappy-looking hawk. The sun was hot, the grass dry and warm. Skylarks sang, white clouds drifted above. Down by the brook, a green woodpecker called. The hawk looked up at the sky, shifted his feet about, looked down at the hedge, then flew. He had not seen prey. He flew very lightly, buoyantly, his wings just surfing the breeze. He slanted and jinked upward like a snipe, touching air deftly, delicately, seeking wing-hold on its gliding smoothness.

In the lower slope of the orchard there is a slight hollow where no trees grow and the grass is scanty and short. The ground there is sheltered from the wind, and warm air rises from it. The hawk spread his wings and tail above this hollow, leaned slowly round into a long half-circle, and turned down wind. He drifted away, and higher. Soon he was high and small and black above the northern end of the orchard. After weeks of skulking, of perching and hovering, he was released, afloat, aloft: he had wrenched himself free.

An abrupt and narrow turn, and he was suddenly still, head to wind, a thousand feet up. For five minutes he hung motionless, tensing and flexing his swept-back wings, dark anchor mooring white cloud. He looked down at the orchard beneath him, twisting and turning his head, mobile, menacing, like the head of a snake looking out of a rock. The wind could not move him, the sun could not lift him. He was fixed and safe in a crevice of sky.

Loosened suddenly out into air, he straightened his wings and circled slowly higher. He slowed, steadied, balanced, and again was still. He was a small speck now, like the pupil of a distant eye. Serenely he floated. Then, like music breaking, he began to descend.

He slid forward and down to his left for two hundred feet, and then stopped. After a long still pause, he came down two hundred feet to his right, then stopped. In this vertical zigzag, from wing-hold to wing-hold, he slowly descended the sheer face of sky. There was no hesitation or checking. He simply dropped, and then stopped, as a spider drops on a thread, or a man on a rope. At last the long exhalation of descent was over. He was back in the thick-rinded air of earth.

I thought he would rest, but above open ploughland he rose again, unable to resist the basking warmth of the sky. Very slowly he rose, for he was still unpractised. His wings strained out and spread to their utmost, his head stretched forward, his eyes looked upward. After the first wide circle he knew he was safe. He relaxed, and looked down again. Under a big white cloud he wound away northward, dwindling up in his long sweeping circles. But he was reluctant to leave the orchard and he would not keep with the cloud. He glided slowly back, through a thousand feet of sunlit air, to perch in a tree near the brook. There he rested, after forty minutes of flight, but he did not sleep. When I went closer, he did not notice me. He did not look at anything. His eyes were open, but unfocused. He flew south, moving like a sleepwalker, gazing forward enrapt. His wings just touched and skimmed the air. The sun shone upon him, and he gleamed like a shield of silver water, glowed purple-brown and wet like dark ploughland after rain.

Beyond the line of poplars, he circled and began to soar again. This time he pulled across the wind, rising swiftly to the north-west, moving far out and very high above the river valley. Gliding, spiralling, hovering, sculling, he seemed to be freed at last from his orchard obsession. Free! You cannot know what freedom means till you have seen a peregrine loosed into the warm spring sky to roam at will through all the far provinces of light. Along the escarpments of the river air he rose with martial motion. Like a dolphin in green seas, like an otter in the startled water, he poured through deep lagoons of sky up to the high white reefs of cirrus. When my arms were aching, and I could watch him no longer, he blurred into a tiny speck and vanished from the bright circle of my vision. Soon I found him again, and saw him grow larger. Gradually, steadily, he grew larger. From thousands of feet above the valley he was diving back to the orchard, which he was not yet ready to leave completely. He grew from a speck to a blur, to a bird, to a hawk, to a peregrine; a winged head shouldering down through the wind. With a rush, with a flash, with a whirr of wings, he came down to the hedge ten yards away from me. He perched, he preened, he looked around; not tired, not tested even, by his half-hour of festive flight. With the whole valley to choose from, he had chosen to come back to the orchard where I was standing. There is a bond: impalpable, indefinable, but it exists.

It is now four o'clock. The sun is still warm, the sky almost cloudless. The tiercel looks upward. Following his gaze, I see a falcon circling over from the east. In the purity of sunlight, her clenched feet, and the pale feathers above them, gleam out in ivory and gold. The whole bird shines with a solid Aztec radiance, as though it were cast in bronze, not buoyant and feathery and hollow-boned. She saw the tiercel circling, and has come from the estuary to join him. That was the purpose of his flight. He rises from the orchard, and together they float slowly overhead, drifting, drifting and calling. Their harsh calls strike hard on the flinty sky. Peregrines often call when they first come to their winter home and again when they leave it. Slowly their slack circles tighten. Soon they are circling at great speed, one high above the other. In long sweeping arcs they rise away to the south-east, fast glides alternating with many deep, chopping wing-beats. There is urgency and strength in every movement. The sun and wind command them no longer. They have their own power, and know their course at last.

Now they can see the coast of Holland, a hundred miles away. They can see the winding mouths of the Scheldt, the white line of the dykes, and the far glitter of the Rhine, standing in the shadow of the night to come. They are leaving the familiar pattern of woods and fields, rivers and coloured farms: leaving the estuary, its green islands and the never ceasing movement of its serpent mud; leaving the tawny outgrowths of the saltings, the sudden straightness of the coastline, the sharp sunlit edges of the land. These vivid images shrink into a rainbow of crushed colour, and set below the horizon of their memory. Other images arise, as yet like mirages distorted, to be made clear in the long whiteness of the continental coast, in far islands now in darkness, in cliffs and mountains sailing out from night.

March 29th. Two hundred golden plover fed in growing corn, listening and stabbing forward and down, like big thrushes.

Many were already in summer plumage. Their black chests shone in the sun below the mustard yellow of their backs, like black shoes half covered with buttercup dust. On the river bank I found the remains of a hare. It had been dead for several days. Fur had been plucked from the exposed bones. Some of the thinner bones had triangular pieces nipped out of them by a peregrine's bill. It may have been found dead and eaten, but it is much more likely that it was killed by two peregrines hunting together. I have found hares like this before, usually in March, when moulting peregrines kill many mammals.

Robins sang in a wood near the river, clear as spring water, fresh as the curled, crisped heart of a lettuce. Like the tinkle of a harpsichord, their song has a misty brightness of nostalgia. The wood smelt of bark and ashes and dead leaves. Circles of cold sky shone at the end of rides. A cock bullfinch squatted on a sagging larch twig. He stretched his neck up towards the twig above him, bit off a bud with a delicate snip and twist of his bill, and chewed it ruminatively. Then he hung his head downwards and snipped off buds from a lower twig. He was a red and black fatty, idly grazing, occasionally exerting himself to breathe out the husky 'du-dudu' of his song, fat dewlap gently quivering. He was like a munching bullock feeding on hawthorn leaves. But the pull and twist of his bill to break off a bud reminded me of a peregrine breaking the neck of its prey. Whatever is destroyed, the act of destruction does not vary much. Beauty is vapour from the pit of death.

I went to the brook to look for the golden tiercel. I had not seen him in the valley since the 24th. At one o'clock a kestrel hovered above the fields near South Wood. His wings flicked the wind gingerly, like fingers lightly touching a hot iron. They quivered up and down like the blade of a ham knife. He dropped lower, and stayed still, wings bent back from the carpal joints, their pale edges flashing in the sun. Then he plunged vertically, parachuting down with bent wings streaming above. (Kestrels do not fold their wings to their sides when diving, as peregrines do.) He levelled out at the last moment, and thudded onto something hidden in the grass. It hung limp and grey from his bill as he flew to a mole-hill to eat it. When I moved towards him, he went at once, leaving his prey behind. It was a common shrew, very small and light The impressions of the kestrel's gripping toes still showed on its soft grey fur. I replaced it on the molehill, hoping the hawk would come back for it when I had gone.

For two hours I waited under the wych elm near the dead tree, but the peregrine did not appear. A curious bleating sound began in the sky above me, very faint at first, gradually becoming louder. It was a snipe drumming. I looked for him at fifty feet, but found him eventually at nearer five hundred. Small as a lark, he circled very fast, covering a large area. He shone and twinkled in the sun, or cut across white clouds like a black diamond. Every twenty seconds he tilted into a shallow dive and spread his tail feathers wide apart so that the air beating against them made that curious comb-and-tissue-paper bleating sound, which is called drumming. There were eight to ten distinguishable buzzing notes, the fourth or fifth being the loudest. They rose to a crescendo, then died away as the snipe resumed his level circling. The sound was astonishingly loud and vibrant. It was like a succession of giant arrows thrumming violently overhead. It was an ominous sound, as though an oracle was about to speak from the sky. It gave me the feeling of having nowhere to hide. After circling and drumming for five minutes, the snipe dropped to the marshy ground near the brook. There are always snipe there in March, if the water-level is high, but they never remain to breed.

Half an hour later, drumming began again. The snipe

circled till he was even higher than before, till he was only just visible. As I watched him I saw what I took to be a second snipe, circling lower down. But in binoculars I recognised it at once as the tiercel peregrine. He rose quickly towards the snipe, which was not aware of danger till the hawk was within fifty feet of him. Then his drumming stopped and he began to jink up at a steep angle, as he does when flushed from the ground. The hawk toiled after him. The snipe flew downwards but the hawk stooped at once and forced him to climb again. This manœuvre was repeated ten or eleven times, till both birds were almost hidden in the upper sky. They towered to a great height above the river, where I expected the almost exhausted snipe to make his last effort to escape by dropping down into a reed-bed. He fell quite suddenly, as though he had been struck. He tumbled vertically down. The hawk slanted down more smoothly, cutting in towards him. Five hundred feet above the river the two silhouettes merged into one dark bird, which rose again, and came slowly back to the brook. The tiercel took his prey to the dead elm. He plucked and ate it there, while sunlight glowed his feather-rippling back to the colour of golden wheat. He rested after feeding, then flew east towards his roosting tree, a solitary elm on one of the estuary islands.

March 30th. Rain fell till two o'clock, followed by showers and mist and watery sunlight. I found the peregrine at three, perched in an elm near North Wood. He was large and puffy with moisture, and he would not fly far. A tremendous gust of rain blew over at half past three. The peregrine faced it till he was drenched, then he flew to a hollow tree and crept inside, out of the wind. When the rain stopped, he flapped slowly and heavily down to a field of stubble where sparrows were feeding. They did not scatter till he plunged among them. He caught one easily and carried it up to the elm to eat. His slow, heavy flight was just like a crow's, and the sparrows were deceived by it.

The sun came out, and the hawk began to dry his dripping feathers. A storm swelled up from the south. I lost sight of the hawk in the crackling gloom. Rain fell from a purple cloud, and the wind rose to a gale. A stoat ran past me, leaping with the lightning flashes. He carried a dead mouse in his jaws.

When the rain lifted, mist rose from the drenched grass. Everywhere there was the ripple and bubble of the lost rain seeking its stillness in the slow river water. The hawk had gone. Little owls lamented in the early dusk.

March 31st. It was a cool limpid sunrise, just a lightening of the eastern haze, a faint intensity of cloud. A late barn owl wavered by the river, white above a black reflection. The peregrine glided over, swooped at the quiet owl. Reflections swayed and clashed, like a rush of pike-torn water. The owl dodged as nimbly as a lapwing, but it flew much faster; slashes of flake white glimmered across green fields. The peregrine lifted from the chase, soared in the first sunlight, circled east; the owl crept to darkness in a hollow tree.

Two lesser spotted woodpeckers flew into a grove of larches. I heard their strident, slightly muffled calls. The slurred, breathy notes were exhaled with effort; a querulous, strangulated neighing. They perched on a high larch twig, a foot apart, hissing and buffeting each other with their wings. Then they retreated into ballet attitudes. They stood erect, with leaf-shaped wings held open to show the wavy markings on the pale undersides, pointing their bills vertically upward. They looked like strange primeval butterflies clinging to a huge tree-fern in a steamy prehistoric jungle. One flew to a dead willow. He landed on the side of the tree, without loss of speed, as though his large feet were disced with suckers.

White bars shone across the darkness of his elliptical, lady-bird back, which always looks as if a small white-painted ladder had been leant against it, leaving wet rung marks. He drummed on the dead wood in long rattling sequences, with only short pauses between them. His bill bounced back too fast for the individual taps to be seen; the shuddering head was blurred. His drumming is a little slower than the great spotted woodpecker's. It is pitched higher, and it does not die away. With practice, the two can always be distinguished. The ear learns quicker than the eye.

After drumming, he tapped on the tree a dozen times, slowly, emphatically, and very loudly, drawing his head so far back that he had to lean outwards to the full extent of his legs. The second bird came bounding across, and landed on the other side of the tree. Both were still for a minute. Then the second bird fluttered aggressively at the other, and drove him off, taking his place at the sounding-board. When the lesser spotted woodpecker's drumming is prolonged, it has a slight resemblance—both in resonance and vibration—to the song of a nightjar. Undoubtedly the sound is mechanically produced, by the stuttering rattle of the bill against dead wood, but it may also echo against the bird's syrinx in some way. That could explain the incredible loudness of the sound. The loudest drumming is produced with the tips of the mandibles held wide apart.

Willow warblers and chiff-chaffs sang softly in the faint green mist of the hill woods. The big head of a tawny owl bobbed across the gloomy gaps of light in a fir plantation. Where the sun shone, there were blue shadows fumed with a humming warmth of insects. Down through the trees, I could see the small fields, and the dark indentation of the river. The peregrine appeared, stooping at a gull. They passed like a moving film, flicking behind trees, then snapping off into darkness.

The estuary was quiet; no hawks, no kills. A pair of lap-wings called across the marshes, the hen in the grass, the cock singing and displaying. He flew like a mad clown, whirling orange, black, and white. His wings seemed to cartwheel along the ground, like windmill sails walking. They flexed like fins, waved like tentacles, as he tumbled, swooped, and climbed, tangling with the air.

April 2nd. Spring evening; the air mild, without edges, smelling of damp grass, fresh soil, and farm chemicals. There is less bird-song now. Many of the singing birds of March were migrants, and have gone back to the north. Most of the black-birds and skylarks have gone, but a hundred fieldfares still roost in trees by the river. Reed buntings have come back to their nesting territories. The white rumps of wheatears star the dark brown ploughland. Two peregrine kills lie beside the river. Both are woodpigeons. One is hardly touched; light still shines with an intense, fanatic blueness from its fish-like eyes. The other has been remarkably well eaten. It is deep in a reed-bed, near a huge pile of plucked feathers; just a husk of hollow bones.

A swallow flits past, purple against the roaring whiteness of the weir, blue over the green smoothness of the river. As so often on spring evenings, no birds sing near me, while all the distant trees and bushes ring with song. Like all human beings, I seem to walk within a hoop of red-hot iron, a hundred yards across, that sears away all life. When I stand still, it cools, and slowly disappears. Seven o'clock. Under elms and hawthorns it is already dusk. A bird flies low across the field, coming straight towards me. It skims over the long grass, like an owl. The deep keel of its breast-bone actually touches and parts the grass as it comes. Its wings beat easily, fanning high, their tips almost meeting above its back. Its head is broad and owl-like. There is a wonderfully exciting softness and silent stealth in its fast approach across the shadowed field. It is looking down into the grass, and only occasionally glancing up to see where it is going. As it comes nearer, I can see that it is a hunting peregrine, a tiercel, trying to flush partridges by flying very low.

He sees me and swerves to his right, swings up to perch in a big wych elm. The last pale sunlight shines on his broad back, which gleams like cloth of gold. He is alert, avid, never still. Soon he dives smoothly down and flickers erratically away to the north-east. He lands on an overhead cable, out in the open fields, and stays there for fifteen minutes. He is very upright and watchful, a bulky silhouette in the fading light, looking back over his left shoulder. Then he flies low and fast across ploughland and behind trees, accelerating with long cleaving wing-strokes. Spring dusk; creak of bats' wings over the steel river, curlew-call of the lemuring owls.

April 3rd. It was warm. The wind slowly lifted the sunlit haze of morning. Clouds formed, but broke again to blue. A noctule bat flew above the river for half an hour, hawking for insects and occasionally calling. The sun shone on its fuzzy brown back, and showed up its long furry ears. I could not find the peregrine.

Great spotted woodpeckers were noisy in South Wood. Seven sailed out of a tree together, chittering like piglets. They separated, and floated away on stiffly outstretched wings. They settled on the surrounding trees, and drummed for a second before dispersing; glorious clowns in Arden. A great spotted woodpecker's drumming has a rich hollow sound if the texture of the wood is right. He looks at the tree for a moment, then leans slowly back and tilts quickly forward. After the initial blow, the others follow in a rapid volley. The bill seems merely to rebound from the wood, like a ball bouncing less and less. The taps get steadily softer and the bill closer and closer, till in the end it is almost resting against the tree, and the drumming dies away. He waits for a reply. He may wait for twenty minutes in the same position. When he hears drumming, he answers it at once.

A nuthatch scuttled across beech bark, well concealed until the rich 'quee, quee, quee, quee' of his song rang out. His back matches the bark, his breast is the colour of a dead beech leaf. He also sang a loud high-pitched trill, a shivering mechanical sound, like a woodpecker drumming on a triangle.

In early April, wherever there are hornbeams there are flocks of singing greenfinches. Many were droning and purring drowsily in the sunlit coppice of North Wood. Some were feeding in the deep leaf-mould, with chaffinches, great tits, a marsh tit, and a robin. Frequently the flock flew up to the trees with a dry rustle of wings, then drifted silently down again through the dust-moted trellis of sun and shade. The yellow sunlight flickered with a thin drizzle of bird shadow. Flocked birds seem to be threaded on one huge nerve. They react extravagantly to the slightest change of light or movement. Suddenly I saw a hawfinch among them, bulky and masterful, a boar of a bird, with a heavy yellow bill like the prow of an icebreaker. He called: a loud emphatic 'tsink,' a hiss and a pop and a whistle, all combined. I looked for him again, but could not find him. I did not see him come. I did not see him go. Like other belligerent-looking birds, hawfinches are wary and timid.

The thick scent of bluebells mingled with the smell of sulphur drifting from the orchard. A cuckoo flew slowly up from the direction of the river, following the windings of the brook. He came into the wood, and began his two months of unwearying song. Even if one is very close and can see him clearly, the two notes of his song seem to come from far away inside him. They are still muffled, as they were at a distance. He sings with an insane concentration. His eye has a fishy glaze. Its orange-yellow iris looks like a coloured bead pinned to his head. He is a tiresome lecherous bird, forever singing and listening for the bell-like ululation of his mate. After feeding in the wood he flew out across the fields, and was immediately chased by the peregrine, who may have been waiting for him, having heard and identified his song. He dodged back into the wood, and did not leave it again. Most hawks kill and eat cuckoos whenever they can, possibly because they find them easy to catch.

I followed the peregrine—it was the golden-coloured tiercel —across to the dead elm, where he rested for an hour, watching the sky, At five o'clock he circled up in wide rings and began to soar. He drifted east, calling and looking down. He called for a long time, as the hawk that departs calls down his sorrow to the one that stays. Then he glided away towards the coast. Slowly his speed increased. He was travelling on an immense parabola, and long before his final vertical fall was ended he had vanished into the hard clear light of the eastern sky.

A green woodpecker called and flew high above the open fields. A jay flew from tree to tree, crossing warily between the two woods; the first I had seen away from cover since October. Long-tailed tits flitted down from the hedges to collect feathers for their nests from kills the peregrine had made. These birds knew, as I knew, that the last peregrine had left the valley. They possessed the freedom I had lost.

April 4th. Wild cherry lined the green lane to the creek with the green and white of leaf and blossom. Bullfinches puffed out black and white and scarlet, flashed, and vanished into husky calling. Colour faded to the brim of water, and the land ended.

The sky was grey, but brightness floated in upon the tide. Larks sang. It was the best of the day. Dusk was already moving through the distant trees and hedges. The creeks and bays were quiet and undisturbed. The songs and calls of birds blended with the sway and ripple of the tide. I had come there to search for the peregrine. It had been late when he left the valley the previous evening, and I thought he might pause to hunt along the coast before migrating. The wind had backed to the north and the day was damp and cold. But the estuary was too peaceful, the birds too much at ease. The calm and empty sky was hawkless. On the sea-wall I found the body of a carrion crow. A peregrine had killed it not many hours before. Black feathers wreathed its bloodstained bones. Its grim, skull-cracking, eye-piercing bill pointed to the sky. It was a head and wings.

At three o'clock I suddenly felt sure that, if I went at once to the coast, eight miles away, I should find the peregrine there. Such certainty comes seldom, but when it comes it is as irresistible as the downward bending of the dowser's twig. I went.

It seemed hopeless. Dark clouds gloomed low in the cold north wind, and the light was very bad. The falling tide was far out across the saltings. The fields were as grey and bleak as the distant sea. Land and sea had been beaten flat into the same dull toneless metal. I love the desolate, but this was beyond desolation. It was dead.

A shelduck lay on the mud, shining like a broken vase; green-black and white, chestnut-bronze, vermilion. Feathers had been plucked from its breast, flesh had been sliced from the bone; deep down inside, the blood was wet. The peregrine had fed; was he still near? I clambered up the side of the sea-wall and looked cautiously over the top.

He was there, less than a hundred yards away, perching on an overhead wire, outlined against the dark inland sky. He must have flown there while I was hidden behind the wall. He faced the wind, waiting for night, drowsy and unwilling to move. A corn bunting flew up beside him, and squeezed out its parched and feeble song. When I went closer, the bunting flew, but not the hawk. At twenty yards he began to look uneasy. He drifted lightly from the wire, flexed his wings once, turned, and glided down wind. I ran along the path beside the wall and saw him alighting on a fence-post on the inland side of the dyke. As I approached, he moved farther inland, flitting from post to post. When the fence ended, he flew across to a small thorn bush on the far side of the old sea-wall.

Screened by the low green bank of the wall, I stumble along on my hands and knees towards the place where I think the hawk will be, hoping he will stay there till I come. The short grass is dry and brittle and sweet-smelling. It is spring grass, clean and sharp as salt water. I bury my face in it, breathe in it, breathe in the spring. A snipe flies up, and a golden plover. I lie still till they have gone. Then I move forward again, very softly, because the hawk is listening. Slowly the dusk begins to uncoil. Not the short wild pang of winter dusk, but the long slow dusk of spring. Mist stirs in the dykes and furs the edges of the fields. I have to guess where I am in relation to the hawk. Three more yards, and I decide to take a chance. Very slowly I straighten up and look over the top of the wall. I am lucky. The hawk is only five yards away. He sees me at once. He does not fly, but his feet grip tightly on the thorny twigs of the bush, the ridged knuckles tense, and big with muscle. His wings loosen, and tremble at the edge of flight. I keep still, hoping he will relax, and accept my predatory shape that bulks against the sky. The long feathers of his breast are rippled by the wind. I cannot see his colour. In the falling gloom he looks much larger than he really is. The noble head lowers, but lifts again at once. Swiftly now he is resigning his savagery to the night that rises round us like dark water. The great eyes look into mine. When I move my arm before his face, they still look on, as though they see something beyond me from which they cannot look away. The last light flakes and crumbles down. Distance moves through the dim lines of the inland elms, and comes closer, and gathers behind the darkness of the hawk. I know he will not fly now. I climb over the wall and stand before him. And he sleeps.

OTHER NEW YORK REVIEW CLASSICS

For a complete list of titles, visit www.nyrb.com or write to:
Catalog Requests, NYRB, 435 Hudson Street, New York, NY 10014

J.R. ACKERLEY My Dog Tulip*
RENATA ADLER Speedboat*
AESCHYLUS Prometheus Bound; translated by Joel Agee*
CÉLESTE ALBARET Monsieur Proust
KINGSLEY AMIS Lucky Jim*
U.R. ANANTHAMURTHY Samskara: A Rite for a Dead Man*
WILLIAM ATTAWAY Blood on the Forge
W.H. AUDEN (EDITOR) The Living Thoughts of Kierkegaard
ERICH AUERBACH Dante: Poet of the Secular World
EVE BABITZ Eve's Hollywood*
S. JOSEPHINE BAKER Fighting for Life*
HONORÉ DE BALZAC The Human Comedy: Selected Stories*
VICKI BAUM Grand Hotel*
SYBILLE BEDFORD A Legacy*
MAX BEERBOHM The Prince of Minor Writers: The Selected Essays of Max Beerbohm*
FRANS G. BENGTSSON The Long Ships*
ALEXANDER BERKMAN Prison Memoirs of an Anarchist
ADOLFO BIOY CASARES The Invention of Morel
RONALD BLYTHE Akenfield: Portrait of an English Village*
NICOLAS BOUVIER The Way of the World
ROBERT BRESSON Notes on the Cinematograph*
SIR THOMAS BROWNE Religio Medici and Urne-Buriall*
ROBERT BURTON The Anatomy of Melancholy
J.L. CARR A Month in the Country*
LEONORA CARRINGTON Down Below*
EILEEN CHANG Naked Earth*
JEAN-PAUL CLÉBERT Paris Vagabond*
RICHARD COBB Paris and Elsewhere
JOHN COLLIER Fancies and Goodnights
IVY COMPTON-BURNETT Manservant and Maidservant
BARBARA COMYNS The Vet's Daughter
ASTOLPHE DE CUSTINE Letters from Russia*
ELIZABETH DAVID Summer Cooking
MARIA DERMOÛT The Ten Thousand Things
TIBOR DÉRY Niki: The Story of a Dog
ANTONIO DI BENEDETTO Zama*
ALFRED DÖBLIN Bright Magic: Stories*
CHARLES DUFF A Handbook on Hanging
DAPHNE DU MAURIER Don't Look Now: Stories
G.B. EDWARDS The Book of Ebenezer Le Page*
J.G. FARRELL The Siege of Krishnapur*
FÉLIX FÉNÉON Novels in Three Lines*
M.I. FINLEY The World of Odysseus
MAVIS GALLANT The Cost of Living: Early and Uncollected Stories*
GABRIEL GARCÍA MÁRQUEZ Clandestine in Chile: The Adventures of Miguel Littín
LEONARD GARDNER Fat City*
WILLIAM H. GASS On Being Blue: A Philosophical Inquiry*

* *Also available as an electronic book.*